Sacred Lessons From True

Stay Tender.
Stay True.
Stay You.

Sacred Lessons From True

What Healing from Complex Trauma Taught Me About Life, Love, & Being Human

By Melanie Taylor, LPC-S

Published in the United States by The True Blueprint LLC: ISBN 979-8-9938648-2-2

Cover design and interior book design by Sarah Trahan

For Denelle Taylor,

The first to read all my work, every book and lesson, before I ever shared it with the world. Even when our relationship was marked by silence, and misunderstanding tried to wedge its way in, you still showed up. You read You Are for True in just one day. Then, when it was ready, you read Sacred Lessons from True, too. You felt it all, then offered it back with love, and that mattered more than I knew how to say.

Thank you for being the one who always reads my books first, and for being part of the healing that brought us back.

For Sarah Trahan,

The one who saw my vision and helped bring it to life. You have poured countless hours, so much creativity, and extraordinary care into making this book beautiful. Somehow, you understood what I could see in my mind and found a way to bring it to life on these pages. You caught the details I missed, patiently worked through every change, and continued giving your time and your gifts until this book became everything I hoped it could be.

This may be my story, but your fingerprints are woven throughout every page. I cannot thank you enough for believing in my vision, caring for it as if it were your own, and helping me carry it all the way to the finish line. I truly could not have done this without you.

AUTHOR'S NOTE

When I began writing this book, I wasn't doing it because I had all the answers. I was still trying to remember what was true.

There came a point in my healing when surviving wasn't enough anymore. I wanted to feel, connect, and live from a place that didn't revolve around what I had been through. But when I tried, I realized I didn't know who I was without the trauma. That was when I began to meet the part of me I now call True.

True is the bridge between my spirit and my soul. She is the light I came into this world with, the one I spent decades trying to earn, only to discover she had never left me. These sacred lessons are the truths she taught me. Some came gently. Others came through trials by fire. Over time, each one became part of my return to myself.

If you carry wounds around worth, love, shame, boundaries, grief, or voice, I hope these pages give you language for what your body already knows. I hope they help you uncover the parts of yourself that trauma taught you to hide and remind you that they are still there, waiting for you.

I don't know exactly where this book will find you. But I do know this:

You are not behind.

You are not too much.

And you are still worth the return.

Stay tender. Stay true. Stay you.

Melanie

CONTENTS

ABOUT TRUE

Who is True?

Think of True as my truest self, the part of me who has always known I was created to be loved because I came from love.

She is the part of me that never left, even when I did. She held the light when I went into hiding and remembered who I was all the times trauma tried to make me forget. She isn't a persona, a concept, or a voice outside of me. She is the calm, steadfast presence within me, the place where my divine spark meets my human pain.

For much of my life, I couldn't find her. I was too busy surviving, performing, and disappearing. I mistook adaptation for strength and silence for peace. But when the ache of being disconnected from myself became too loud to ignore, I began to listen. Beneath everything I had learned to be, I heard a whisper leading me home. That whisper was True.

True never shamed the ways I had survived. She simply helped me remember what trauma had taught me to forget: I was never meant to carry everything alone, and I had never stopped being worthy of finding my way back to myself.

True belongs to my story, but I believe there is something within each of us that remembers who we were before the world told us who we needed to become. As you read these pages, I hope you begin to recognize that place within yourself. It may be quiet. It may have been hidden for a long time. But it is still there.

HOW TO READ THIS BOOK

Sacred Lessons from True is organized into themes, each containing lessons shaped by my own healing and the experiences that taught me how to live differently.

Each theme begins with a short reflection. The lessons that follow include personal stories, the truths I discovered within them, a Sacred Pause, and a reminder of what you are for.

This is not a step-by-step guide, and you do not have to read it that way. You can begin at the beginning, or you can turn to the lesson that feels most relevant to where you are right now. Some lessons may meet you gently. Others may stir emotions you need time to sit with. Take your time. Put the book down when you need to. Return when you are ready. Linger wherever something feels important.

There are no rules for moving through these pages. There is only an invitation to notice which truths feel familiar, which ones challenge you, and which ones you may be ready to carry with you.

Let this book meet you exactly where you are.

Sacred Theme One

Remembering Your Worth

Sacred Theme One:
Remembering Your Worth

There are truths we are born knowing: that we're good, that we belong, that we're loved simply because we exist. But somewhere along the way, those truths can become buried beneath criticism, silence, or the weight of what others cannot see in us because they cannot see it in themselves.

A child does not stop needing celebration simply because they are never celebrated. But they may begin to believe they are unworthy of it. When love is given and then taken away, a child continues to long for it but may begin to believe it must be earned, begged for, or performed into existence.

This theme is about returning to what was always yours: your sacred, unshakable worth. It has nothing to do with what you have accomplished, what you can offer others, or what you have survived. You are worthy because you came from love and were created to be loved.

These first lessons invite you to remember who you were before the world told you who you were supposed to be, before shame changed your reflection and you learned to hide what was sacred within you.

You do not have to prove anything to return to your worth. You only have to begin remembering what trauma taught you to forget.

- Your Worth Is Not up for Debate
- You Were Created to Be Loved
- You Were Created to Be Celebrated
- The Healing Process Was Never Meant to Be Carried Alone

Sacred Lesson from True:
Your Worth Is Not Up for Debate

Worthiness isn't something you earn. It isn't a grade, a role, a title, or a performance. It isn't granted by others or revoked when you fall short. Worth is intrinsic. It lives in your breath, your heartbeat, and your being. You are worthy simply because you exist, because you were born, and because you are here. No amount of rejection, neglect, or cruelty can undo that truth. But I didn't always know that.

For a long time, I confused worth with value to others. Being valuable to the people around me was how I survived. I learned early that value was visible and measurable. It meant being helpful, quiet, conciliatory, and pleasing. I needed to earn good grades, remain strong no matter what, and stay small enough to keep the peace. But what made me valuable seemed to change constantly depending on who was watching, what they wanted, and how well I could meet their needs. It was a moving target. Worth, in contrast, is still, sacred, and unbothered by the world's noise.

I believed that if I wasn't valuable to others, I wasn't worthy. If I didn't perform or couldn't earn love, then I didn't deserve it. But I didn't invent that belief on my own. It had been passed down through generations. In families shaped by the need to survive, value becomes currency. Love is conditional, safety is earned, and praise is rare and fleeting. Intrinsic worth isn't even part of the vocabulary.

Generational trauma doesn't teach us about worth; it only teaches us to be useful. We learn to stay small enough to avoid punishment, smart enough not to be shamed, helpful enough not to be hurt, and quiet enough not to be abandoned. When that is the only language of love we have ever known, we begin to believe it is all there is.

But value is a survival metric. It shifts, bends, and wears you out. Worth is different. Worth is eternal. When you grow up in a lineage of suffering, you may be taught that self-sacrifice is love, your needs matter less than everyone else's survival, giving more makes you good, and having more makes you selfish. You learn to measure yourself by what you are willing to give up:

your sleep, your dreams, your voice, your body, or your joy. If your life expands beyond what others have allowed themselves, you may even feel guilty, as though your happiness has broken some silent rule.

So you shrink. You apologize. You pour out every ounce of yourself, hoping someone will call it love. But that isn't love. It is erasure. Sacrifice isn't sacred when it costs you your soul.

When value to others becomes your only language, you begin to speak it with everything you have, even your body. Many times in my life, I didn't know how else to be chosen, so I gave whatever seemed valuable, including touch and access to myself. I wasn't giving from a place of empowerment. I was aching to be seen. I mistook being wanted for being worthy. I told myself that if I could be desirable enough, available enough, or good enough, maybe I would finally feel lovable.

It was never about pleasure. It was about proving I wasn't disposable. Sometimes, for a moment, I felt wanted and important. But the ache always returned. What I truly wanted was not simply to be touched. I wanted to be known, held without having to trade myself in pieces, and told I did not have to give my body away to be worthy of love. Because I did not know how to ask for that, I kept offering what I thought I had to give. Each time, I felt emptier. No one can give back what trauma convinces you to trade away. They cannot return what was never theirs to take.

Perhaps the most painful inheritance is the belief that if you stay long enough, love hard enough, and make yourself small enough, you will finally convince someone to treat you like you matter. This is how we remain in painful patterns, shape-shifting to meet the expectations of people who cannot truly see us. We hide the parts they consider too much, too soft, or too wild and offer only the fragments we think they will accept. We confuse loyalty with worth and surviving with being loved. When it still does not work, we question ourselves instead of questioning the relationship.

The result is a shame so deep that it convinces us we are the reason love keeps slipping through our fingers. But we were never meant to prove our worth by staying where our souls go numb. You do not need someone else to validate your belonging. You are allowed to want more. You are allowed to grieve what you did not receive. You can hold both truths at once: this hurts, and I deserve more.

Sometimes, the bravest thing you can do is to stop trying to be worthy in someone else's eyes and start recognizing the worth that was always yours. Maybe you are starting to feel it now, a flicker of awareness rising from somewhere deep within you. It may still be subtle, but it is there.

Noticing it can be terrifying. When you have hidden something sacred for so long, even glancing toward it can feel dangerous. Naming it can feel like defiance. You may begin to wonder: Who am I if I no longer disappear to make others comfortable? What happens if I let myself be seen?

You want to believe in your worth, but setting boundaries, taking up space, and allowing your truth to be known can feel frightening. That fear makes sense. The worthy self was buried for a reason. You were protecting her. As you allow her to rise, you may feel exposed and uncertain, as though you are walking barefoot through the world for the first time.

You do not need to shout or convince anyone. Stay close to what is true. Keep it warm and let it grow. Not everyone will know how to respond, but that does not mean you need to turn away from yourself. You do not have to disappear to remain connected. Your worth is not up for debate, but your circle is. You get to decide who surrounds you, not so they can prove your worth, but so your relationships reflect it. Not everyone deserves access to what is sacred within you. That is not selfishness. It is sovereignty.

Although I didn't know this truth back then, True always did. She stood behind the shame, the silence, and the survival. She never forgot who I was, even when I did. She never asked me to perform. She only continued calling me back to the self trauma had taught me to hide, the part of me that remembered my name before it was ever associated with pain.

There was a light inside me that the world tried to extinguish. But shame, violence, and neglect could not destroy it because I had been born with it. The world had not given it to me, so the world could not take it away. Even the parts of me that rose in rage, fell silent, or struggled with perfectionism were not failures. They were protectors guarding something sacred until I was ready to find it again.

Learning to love those parts, and learning to love the light they protected, has been some of the greatest work of my life. So if you are reading these words and wondering whether you are worthy, please know that you are. Even now. Especially now. Your worth is not up for debate and never has been. You do not have to perform, become perfect, or wait for someone else to name what has always been true. You only have to begin remembering.

And when you forget, which you will, trust that something within you still remembers. Listen for the softest whisper beckoning you home. You are sacred, and you have always been worth returning to.

Sacred Pause

For the Moment You Begin to Remember

Close your eyes now, if it's safe to do so. Place a hand over your heart, if it feels right. And take a deep breath to come back to yourself. You don't have to have it all figured out. You don't need to leave that relationship today. You don't have to burn it all down to begin again. You only have to remember that worth doesn't have prerequisites.

You're allowed to feel scared and still choose yourself. You're allowed to love people and still leave what harms you. You're allowed to want something better, even if no one ever taught you how to ask for it. This moment is simply about starting to return. And return begins with the smallest knowing: I deserve more than this.

Hold that truth gently and don't forget it.

You are for...

You are for sacred worth.

You are for rising, even if your voice shakes.
You are for becoming, even if no one claps.

You are for choosing yourself without apology.

You are for being seen, without having to perform.
You are for gentleness that doesn't get swallowed.
You are for truth that doesn't cost you your belonging.

You are for love that doesn't punish.

You are for the kind of presence that never asks you to shrink.

You are for you.
You always have been.
And you always will be.

Sacred Lesson from True:
You Were Created to Be Loved

Love is your birthright. You never needed to earn it. You were created to be loved, not tested, proven, or molded into something easier for others to accept. You were created to be cherished simply because you exist.

But many of us didn't grow up in a world that knew how to offer that kind of love. We grew up performing, apologizing, over-functioning, and disappearing. We learned to measure our worth in usefulness, obedience, silence, or smiles. And we came to believe love was a reward we would deserve if we got it right and didn't need too much, or if we were good enough, small enough, or helpful enough.

And so we became hyper-independent and carried everything ourselves. We learned to fix things on our own and to be our own shelter, even when all we wanted was to be held. For many of us, there was no one else. In other cases, depending on someone felt dangerous, or waiting to be loved only led to disappointment, punishment, or silence.

I didn't become strong because I wanted to. I became strong because I had no other choice. I became capable because there was no one to ask for help, and calm because falling apart never felt safe. Underneath that strength was a child who just wanted someone to come near and say, You don't have to do this by yourself anymore.

But sometimes, love arrives. A steady, regulated, gentle kind of love that doesn't yell or demand that you shrink. This kind of love is calm, even when it's hurting, and knows how to stay.

With him, it started slowly. We were just friends for a whole year before anything ever moved forward. That friendship with him was my first sense of safety. He made no demands and exerted no pressure. Early on, I said to him, half-joking, half-serious, "I want the next person I sleep with to be the last one, but not because of a serial killer." He smiled, but he also respected and honored the serious sentiment behind my words.

And later, when we got closer, he paused and said, "I want to make sure you're ready. But more importantly, I need to make sure I am too."

No one had ever said that to me before. His willingness to move slowly felt respectful and sacred. It gave me a corrective experience my body didn't even know it had been longing for.

That love led to a marriage that has been beautiful and steady, but also rocky in ways we couldn't have anticipated. The love was never lacking. We simply didn't fully understand what complex trauma would mean for intimacy, comfort, and connection.

Receiving love was difficult for me at first, even though it was the very thing I'd always longed for. It wasn't easy for me to let someone in or be comforted. Being loved when you've never known safe love is like learning a new language with no translation. You recognize the sounds but don't know how to let them land. You hear the words but can't quite believe they're really meant for you.

But over time, I also learned the true meaning of intimacy. I often tell my clients that intimacy means "into me, I see." It's when I trust you enough to show you the darkest parts of me, the ones I used to hide, silence, or apologize for, knowing that I'll still be okay, that love won't disappear once the mask comes off. That's true intimacy. That's what I was always meant for.

And that level of connection, of allowing someone to truly see inside, is something therapy offers too. Therapy is a sacred, one-sided intimacy in a space where you're allowed to be known without having to perform or take care of the person listening. You can say the hardest things out loud and still be met with care. In this space, you get to let the room hold your truth, so this truth can begin to guide you, gently and lovingly, back to yourself.

The reality is that you didn't have to become anything different to deserve love. You never needed to shrink to be wanted or force yourself to be easy, quiet, helpful, or happy to be worthy. You were worthy even in the womb. You were worthy in spite of the messes you've made over the years and in the moments no one saw. And you're still worthy now.

You were born sacred, with a light inside you that was never meant to be dimmed. You were created to be loved. Your worth isn't defined by what you had to survive or measured by how quickly you recovered, how strong you stayed, or who did or didn't love you well.

You're not too much. You're not too late. And most importantly, you're not unlovable.

You're learning how to receive what has always been yours.

And every moment that you let love stay, let love hold you, and let love in, you're not just healing, you're also coming home to who you've always been and what you were truly created for: sacred love. This kind of love sees you, stays with you, and brings you back to this truth.

You were created to be loved. That truth was written into you from the very beginning.

Sacred Pause

For the Ones Learning to Let Love In

Take a breath. It doesn't need to be a perfect one, or a very deep one. Just a breath that says, I'm still here. Place a hand on your chest or belly, wherever you feel the rhythm of your aliveness. Let it remind you that your presence is here. You are here. You don't have to be anyone else to deserve love in this moment.

Now, look back briefly at your past, not to relive it but to honor the difficult things you've carried and the silence you've endured. You've survived more than most people will ever understand. You've adapted, hardened yourself, disappeared, and tried your best. And even through all of that, you were still created to be loved. You weren't made to be loved for what you did or for how strong you stayed, but because love was what you deserved from the beginning.

So pause now, for this moment, and just exist. Don't try to fix anything or do anything to earn love. Just let love find you. Let it feel like the sun landing softly on your face and sound like your name spoken gently close to your ear. Let it be a presence that asks nothing from you but to stay. This is the kind of love that knows how to remain.

In this pause, say: I am learning to let love in.
Even here. Even now. Even me.

You are for...

You are for love that doesn't leave.

You are for warmth that finds the coldest parts of you and stays until they're comforted.

You are for the kind of safety that doesn't flinch when you fall apart.

You are for tenderness that doesn't ask you to earn it.

You are for sacred connection that asks for nothing but your presence.

You are for slow mornings and steady hands.
For the kind of intimacy that says, *Show me what hurts, and I won't run.*

You are for being seen, fully and completely, and loved more, not less, because of it.
For trust that builds like layers of soft blankets, one gentle moment at a time.

You are for tears that don't have to be hidden, and stories that are safe to speak aloud.

You are for resting.
You are for healing.
You are for choosing gentleness without fear.

You are for the sacred return, to your breath, to your truth, to the love that was always yours.

You are for the kind of love that wraps around your becoming and whispers: *You were created to be loved.*

Sacred Lesson from True:
You Were Created to Be Celebrated

There's a difference between being celebrated and feeling celebrated. For a long time, I didn't know that. People would offer me kind words, show up for events, and send cards, but something inside me couldn't take any of it in. It usually felt awkward and distant, like it was meant for someone else. I could see a celebration, but could never feel it.

Growing up, I was taught that we weren't supposed to be too proud of ourselves. Pride was treated as sinful, a sign that someone thought too highly of themselves or had forgotten their place. I learned to minimize my accomplishments, brush off compliments, and make sure I never appeared too pleased with myself. What I didn't understand was how proud of myself I was allowed to be.

Then one day, I looked up the word pride and saw self-love listed as a synonym. It felt as though cold water had been splashed across my face. I had spent so much of my life believing that being proud of myself was sinful or wrong, only to discover that healthy pride could be an expression of self-love. It could mean recognizing what I had survived, honoring what I had accomplished, and allowing myself to feel joy about the person I was becoming.

That realization helped me understand what happened on my forty-ninth birthday. A few close friends came over for a game night, bringing cards, gifts, and laughter. And something else that I wasn't even looking for: their presence. They weren't just there next to me; they were there with me.

After they left, I stood in my kitchen and read through their notes again. I looked at the gifts and let myself pause. And for the first time, I felt it in my body, not just in my mind. I felt celebrated.

As I made this realization, the tears began to fall. I'd been celebrated, and nothing within me had resisted it. I hadn't brushed it off or explained it away. I'd accepted it, and it was glorious. I allowed myself to feel proud, cherished, and loved.

That's when a new truth hit me: celebration isn't as much about attention as recognition. It's about being seen without needing to earn it.

Trauma doesn't just take away safety; it also robs you of delight. It teaches you that joy is fragile, goodness comes with a price, and being treasured is something you have to chase. It convinces you that you're only worthy of being tolerated, not cherished. That you're meant only to survive, not to shine.

But True has been teaching me that we were created for celebration rather than for performance, perfection, or pretending everything's fine. You were created to be celebrated simply because you exist.

Now, I'm learning to honor the parts of me that once hid in shame, carried too much, and never felt like they belonged, believing that love had to be earned. I picture these parts as graduates who have traversed hardships, achieved freedom, and entered into the light. And I smile at them because they made it. They carried things they should never have had to bear, and still, they brought me here.

I'm learning that celebrating myself doesn't mean believing I'm better than anyone else. It means allowing myself to recognize how far I've come without apologizing for it. Healthy pride doesn't place me above anyone else. It allows me to stand beside myself with love.

We weren't created for trauma. We were created for love and laughter, for weird inside jokes and dancing in the kitchen, and for cards that say you matter without needing a reason. We were created to be seen just as we are, quirky, unfinished, and radiant.

We were created to be celebrated.

Sacred Pause

For the Ones Not Used to Being Celebrated

Take a breath. Let it come in slowly and remember that you can take all the time you need. Now place a hand over your heart. Exhale, and then as your chest rises again, let your heart remember what it's been through, and let it now prepare to receive something good.

Whisper to yourself: "I am allowed to be seen and honored. I am allowed to feel joy in my own skin."

You never need to earn celebration or justify your joy. You never have to dim your light just to stay safe. This is your invitation to stop ducking when the spotlight finds you, to stop shrinking when someone says, "You matter." Because you do.

You aren't here just to heal, but also to shine, belong, and be celebrated.

And your True is already clapping for you. Let the applause land. Even if it's just one hand on your chest, saying, "You did it."

Let that be enough for today.

You are for...

You are for joy that doesn't need to be explained.

You are for presence that gets to be honored, not hidden.

You are for laughter that lives in your body without shame.

You are for light that doesn't have to shrink to make others comfortable.

You are for being seen, not for what you produce, but for who you are.

You are for delight that lands and lingers.

You are for being told "You matter" and finally believing it.

You are for belonging that doesn't require effort.

You are for the celebration that meets you exactly as you are: unfinished but radiant and real.

You are for the applause of your own becoming.

You are for shining.

You are for being celebrated.

Sacred Lesson from True:
The Healing Process Was Never Meant to Be Carried Alone

I used to think healing was an individual journey, and that if I just worked hard enough, read all the right books, found the right therapist, and fixed all the broken parts of me, I could become whole. Surely, I told myself again and again, if I could push hard enough, cry deeply enough, and bleed honestly enough, I'd get there in the end. Maybe the aching would stop and I could undo what had been done.

But the more I healed, the more I saw that I was never meant to carry this alone. And neither were you.

That's because trauma isn't just personal, but also generational. It's systemic, embedded not only in our bodies but also in our families, classrooms, and churches, and even in the rules and regulations of our society. It hides in silence and thrives in over-functioning. It's in what we normalize, excuse, and spiritualize to avoid feeling what's true. It doesn't begin with just one person, and it doesn't end with one either.

We keep trying to treat collective wounds with individual solutions. We assign one burned-out therapist to help a family of five. We give a child therapy but then send them back to the chaos of their home. We give one teacher thirty students, three trauma histories apiece, and one hour to "make a difference." We teach coping skills but never change the conditions that created the pain in the first place. And then we wonder why people break.

I know, because I almost did.

I was working in community mental health, trying to run a full program without the appropriate staff or enough support or rest. Every therapist I knew carried a caseload of nearly two hundred clients. We were all overworked, all barely breathing. Productivity was both the carrot and the stick: we were praised for our numbers, not our care, and quantity mattered more than quality. If you could keep up, you were seen as strong and dependable, qualities that became your badge of honor.

But behind that praise, I was falling apart. I was so exhausted, I was starting to have suicidal thoughts. I wasn't making detailed plans, but because I'd been wrung dry, certain thoughts were popping into my mind, like *Maybe it would be easier not to be here.* I'd simply cared too much for too long with too little in return.

I finally said this to my therapist, Nick. And in that sacred space of honesty, I realized my entire identity had become helping others. There was no room left for me or my needs as a human.

So I made a decision. I told my boss I needed two weeks off. She reminded me that I didn't have that many days in my allotted paid time off. But something in me had shifted. I gently told her, "If it comes down to needing more time than I have, I understand. But I have to take this time. I'm not okay."

I said it calmly and clearly. For maybe the first time in my life, I let my well-being matter more than the rules. And to my surprise, she didn't push back or fire me. When I look back at it now, I realize that she kept me on because I was contributing something important, although I didn't feel important at the time.

I stopped seeing clients and started doing only intakes, working just enough hours to survive. It was an act of reclamation in support of my survival. And slowly, over the course of a year, I let myself heal. I began to believe I was worthy, not because of what I gave, but simply because I existed.

Eventually, I opened a small private practice of my own, and the light began to return. But I never forgot what almost took me out. The problem, I could now more clearly see, hadn't been a lack of strength or resilience on my part. I'd just been working in a system that fed on burnout and blamed those who couldn't keep up. It expected us to hold the pain of hundreds while offering us pizza and doughnut parties as thanks.

We can't keep trying to treat trauma inside systems that are themselves built on trauma. We can't heal in places that reward over-functioning and punish grief. And we can't hold others when no one is holding us.

We know more now. We're running out of excuses. We know that trauma changes the brain, and that what goes unnamed and unaddressed becomes the next generation's inheritance. We know that silence isn't safety, and shame isn't discipline. And still, we ask individuals to fix what entire communities have broken.

We must stop assuming people know what trauma is when so many have never been shown what trauma isn't. What finally changed me was a model that showed what childhood was supposed to look like.

It was Erik Erikson's work, of all things, a simple framework with a handful of stages, that opened my eyes. Suddenly, I had language for what I'd missed, a map and a glimpse at what could have been and what still could be.

So no, teaching what trauma looks like isn't enough. We also need to teach what trauma isn't. We need to show people what safety and love feel like, what a sacred "no" sounds like, and what it means to belong in your own body. We need tiny lessons that stretch across a lifetime, guiding people back to their wholeness **and showing them** how to live, love, and fully embody what it means to be a spiritual being having a human experience.

I can't truly see you if all I can see are my own wounds. And you can't see me if all you see is your own pain. We're a nation of the wounded leading the wounded, and no one's seeing what's true.

But no one voice is enough. And no one should have to carry this alone.

True was never meant to be carried alone. But she must be carried inward before she can be carried outward. So we begin with ourselves. And then we begin again, together. Perhaps not perfectly or all at once, but with open hands and eyes that see. We carry what was once unspeakable into the light. We hold each other through the trembling. And we remember.

We remember what we were always meant for. We weren't meant merely for survival, keeping the peace, or carrying weight. We weren't created to numb ourselves, please others, shrink, or endure. We were always meant for healing and we were always worthy of rest. We were always deserving of joy, repair, voice, safety, truth, gentleness, and sacred boundaries. We always deserved laughter that doesn't hurt, and love that doesn't leave.

We were meant to become fully alive. And when we each begin to remember what we're truly for, we start to remember something even deeper: we belong. We belong to ourselves and to each other, to the truth that never left us, a world we are still building, and a love that has always been waiting.

Maybe that's what True was guiding me back to all along. And maybe, if any of this feels familiar to you, she's guiding you as well.

And that is how we begin again.

Sacred Pause

For the Ones Who Have Carried Too Much Alone

Close your eyes, if it's safe, or soften your gaze. Now, feel the breath you've been holding, the one you didn't even realize you were carrying tight in your chest. Let it fall out slowly. This pause isn't meant to be a luxury but a necessary moment of return, a sacred return to your breath, your body, and the truth that you're still here. Even in your unraveling, after you tried to stay strong and push through, some part of you refused to leave.

This pause is for that part of you, the one who kept going when no one noticed, sat in silent rooms and wondered if they'd ever feel light again. The part of you who gave and gave and gave and is just now learning how to receive.

Let this moment hold you. Let it say what no one else knew how to tell you: *You should not have had to carry so much. You were never meant to hold it alone. You are allowed to lay it down now.*

Breathe. Your breath is the proof:

You're still here. And still becoming.

You are for...

You are for breath.
For healing.
For gentleness that holds and strength that doesn't harm.

You are for boundaries that protect your light
and rest that restores your truth.

You are for belonging without performance,
for love that stays,
for truth that is tender
and healing that is shared.

You are not here to be everything for everyone.

You are here to become who you already are:
held, worthy, and whole.

You are for remembering.
You are for returning.

You are for being met with love when you do.

Let this be your breath of power.

Let it say what the world forgot to tell you:
You are enough.
You made it through.

And now, love is guiding you back home.

Sacred Theme Two

Untangling Shame and Honoring Grief

Sacred Theme Two: *Untangling Shame and Honoring Grief*

Some wounds don't show up as bruises, but as silence or apology, or sometimes as excess: over-achieving, over-accommodating, over-everything. And they can show up as shame.

Shame is the voice that says, It was your fault. It's the whisper that turns pain into proof that you're unlovable. But that voice was never True.

This theme is about reclaiming what shame tried to steal: your dignity, your gentleness, and your right to grieve. Grief is something you have a right to feel: it's the natural reaction to losing something that mattered. And guilt, when healthy, can be a guide. But shame only silences.

The following lessons invite you to name what hurt you, honor what you lost, and untangle the lies and shame wrapped around your story. This is where you begin to make space for self-compassion, sacred anger, and the tears that were never allowed to fall.

This is how we return to wholeness: by naming what we were never meant to carry.

- Powerlessness Turns to Rage When Wounds Are Wrapped in Shame
- Shame Loops but Guilt Liberates
- Grief Follows Knowledge
- You Are Allowed to Heal What Someone Else Refused to Repair

Sacred Lesson from True:

Powerlessness Turns to Rage When Wounds Are Wrapped in Shame

There are moments in life that don't announce themselves as wounds. At first, they seem ordinary and harmless. But then something twists inside your chest, because what just happened isn't only what happened. It's also what it touched: something old and tender, something that's still waiting to be healed.

You're walking out of Walmart, with some of the items you just paid for loose in your cart, unbagged. And a woman at the door stops you and says, "I need to see your receipt." You know you paid and didn't do anything wrong. But your chest still tightens, your heart still pounds, and suddenly your body is flooded with heat, shame, and defensiveness.

It doesn't make sense. After all, it's just a store policy, and showing the receipt is easy. But this little moment doesn't feel small to you. It feels like your body knows something it shouldn't have to explain. It feels like a warning: you're not safe, you're not trusted, you're not okay.

And beneath the quick flare of anger, there's something older and heavier. It's more than the shame of this moment; it's also the shame from before. There's an emotional memory of what it felt like to be a child in a world where no one protected you and you were left to carry blame that was never yours. In those days, fear lived in your chest, but there was no one safe enough to talk about it with. And no one ever held you through your pain. No one ever stayed long enough for safety, or True, to take root.

There's a feeling that rises up in these moments, and you've known it your whole life. It's the feeling of being alone, as if you've been pulled into the center of a circle, with every eye on you, watching, judging, and waiting to accuse, to pronounce a verdict you've feared since childhood: you're bad, you're unworthy, and you don't belong. You have to either disappear or defend yourself. Hide or fight. And if you can't do either, you rage.

We've all seen it before. And if we're honest, we've probably all felt it before too. The poor woman working at McDonald's gets an order wrong, and suddenly becomes the target of years of buried fury. This doesn't happen because she forgot the ketchup, but because her mistake may have touched an older experience of feeling unseen, dismissed, or powerless. The mistake is small, but what it touches is not.

Understanding where that reaction comes from doesn't excuse mistreating someone. It helps us recognize what is happening so we can take responsibility for our behavior without covering ourselves in more shame.

This is how a fleeting moment in a fast-food restaurant can turn into fast shame, fast activation, and a fast return to a familiar survival state where you think things like *I'm bad, I'm wrong, and I don't matter.*

This makes us snap and flare. We raise our voice to be heard, but it's also to drown out the pain from years ago that was never resolved.

Or we might do the opposite, smiling politely and saying, "It's fine." We accept the burger that has everything we didn't want on it, the pickles we hate, the sauce we didn't ask for, and we eat it anyway. We silence our voice, convincing ourselves that it's not worth the trouble. We let what we got be enough, even when it wasn't what we wanted or needed.

Somewhere along the way, we learned that asking for what we needed was dangerous, that sending something back, regardless of how nicely we might do it, could invite ridicule or even punishment or abandonment. So we learned to swallow it: the disappointment, discomfort, or desire. And we called it "no big deal."

But our bodies remembered. And so the rage we feel is about all the other times we couldn't say, *This isn't what I asked for. This isn't okay. I deserve better.* And those everyday explosions, or unnoticed swallowings, are the echoes of something deeper.

I didn't always understand this, as the following story shows. Some time ago, my husband and I were shopping for groceries at Walmart, as we always did on Sundays. We would also shop for his dad, who was elderly and legally blind, so our cart was always full. And my husband loved his little bottles of soda. They would sit in our cart like bright, bubbly trophies as we made our way through the store. Since they were already packaged, held together with plastic shrink wrap, we would never put them in a bag at the register but would just place them straight in our trunk.

We'd been doing this for years, and it had always been normal and easy. We had our routine and would always go to the same checkout line with the same cashier. There'd never been any problems, that is not until the day Samantha arrived. Her job was to stand at the door and make sure that departing customers had paid for everything they were taking with them.

Samantha was kind, friendly, and clearly eager to do a good job. But exactly sixty seconds after we checked out, she'd look at our cart, see the unbagged soda bottles, and ask to see our receipt. Every time.

I would always get so angry. I could feel the fire rising in my chest, the weight of shame draped over my shoulders, and the storm of unuttered curse words buzzing in my head. My husband, calm and steady, would sometimes whisper, "If you want to just go sit in the car, it's okay." But I didn't want to sit in the car. I wanted Samantha to stop looking at me like I'd stolen something.

In therapy, I began to see that Samantha wasn't just Samantha. In my mind, she stood for every false accusation I'd ever endured. She brought back every time I'd ever been punished without warning or shamed for something I'd thought I was doing right. She was a symbol of all the times my innocence hadn't protected me, and all the times blame had come before truth. Rage was my only shield when I didn't know how to say, *This isn't mine to carry.*

Eventually, the heat in my chest cooled. I went back to Walmart, a little less rattled, but still uneasy. And one day, talking to our usual cashier, I finally said, "I don't understand why they have to check the receipt when there are cameras everywhere. Why does it always feel like I'm being watched? Like I've done something wrong?"

She smiled and gave me the best advice I've ever gotten at Walmart. She said, "Oh, just take a bag and throw it over the sodas. If there's a bag on it, they can't stop you."

So I did. The next time, I covered those sodas like they were precious cargo. And as we walked out, Samantha looked up, smiled, and said, "Have a good day."

And something shifted. At that moment, I didn't just need to know I wasn't at fault. I needed to feel it. I needed a sacred boundary, something small but real. Something that said, *This is mine. This is true.*

That day, a simple crinkled plastic bag gave me clarity. It wasn't just about sodas; it was also about sovereignty. And it gave me something else: a corrective experience. That's what trauma healing often requires. More than insight, we need new experiences that tell our body a different story, restoring our dignity, agency, and peace. That little bag was one of mine.

It may take me a hundred more bagged sodas before I walk out of Walmart feeling fully at ease. Or maybe I'll decide that naked bottles just aren't worth it and that I deserve the robe of Walmart-bag truth every single time. Either way, that bag gave me something no one else had: a way to protect myself, without apology.

I knew Samantha was doing her job. I also knew that my body experienced the receipt check as an accusation, even when no accusation had been made. Both things could be true. I could honor what the experience touched in me without making her responsible for wounds that were already there.

I don't deserve false accusation, or to be watched like a thief when all I've done is live. I deserve clarity and peace, and to feel safe in my own skin.

When we were young and hurt, and no one came, we learned to split and to hide or defend ourselves. We folded into shame, or we erupted into rage, which is what's left when the vulnerable parts of us never got recognized and no one said, *You're doing so well* or *I see how hard you're trying* or *That wasn't your fault*. You were doing your best in a world that kept punishing you for existing. And even then, you tried to be good.

So now, you make small changes. You take sacred precautions and create boundaries with bags and breath and presence. You teach your body something new. And you walk through the world with a little more safety and clarity. A little more true.

Sometimes, when the heat still rises all the same, you pause and breathe. You remind yourself: *this is not the past. I am not that child. I'm me, now, in the present. And I know what I'm for.*

I am not for shame, whether it's the shame they tried to place on me or the shame I picked up to survive. I am not for the shame that tries to follow me into grocery stores or relationships or ordinary moments that should have stayed small.

I am not for shame in any capacity. I am for truth and tenderness and repair. I am for becoming the safest person I know.

And when I forget, when the heat rises, the sting returns, or the receipt gets demanded, I think of the bag. I remember the boundary and recall that I don't have to be small to be safe. I just have to be whole.

Sacred Pause

For the Ones Who Were Watched, Blamed, or Burned by Shame

Take a breath. Let your body be still for a moment, and remember: you're not in trouble and you don't have to prove anything. You're allowed to be safe. Relax your body and let your shoulders drop. You're not being watched now, but witnessed. There is no guilt here, only grace.

If your body recalls shame more easily than safety, be gentle with that. If you've ever stayed silent when you wanted to speak, or lashed out when you only meant to cry, remember that you're not broken. You're merely wired for protection.

Let this be a moment of sacred unlearning. You don't have to rage to be heard or to disappear to be safe. You don't have to carry shame that was never yours.

You're allowed to come home to yourself without fear, punishment, or pretending.

You are for...

You are for truth without shame.

You are for boundaries that don't require explanations.

You are for saying, *This isn't mine,* and laying it down.

You are for soft courage and sacred clarity.
You are for safe exits and rightful refusals.
You are for peace that doesn't require shrinking.

You are for being seen without suspicion.
Trusted without performance.
Loved without needing to prove your innocence.

You are for holy anger that knows how to pause,
and tenderness that knows when to rise.

You are not for shame.
Not ever. Not again.

You are for truth.

And you are still becoming free.

Sacred Lesson from True:
Shame Loops but Guilt Liberates

Shame isn't always just a feeling. It can also be a full-body collapse. Sometimes it hits like a wave: sudden, overwhelming, and disorienting. Other times, it creeps in slowly, wrapping itself around you until you can't tell where it ends and you begin. Shame isn't felt only in your mind, but in your body, too: you may have a tight chest, a hot face, an aching stomach, and a sudden urge to run away.

Shame doesn't say, *You did something wrong.* It says, *You are something wrong.* It convinces you there's something inherently broken, disgusting, or unworthy about you. And once it takes root in your nervous system, it pops up again in every moment that even slightly resembles an old mistake.

I've lived inside shame storms like that, the kind that make you lose your sense of time and place, when everything feels too loud and too close. In those moments, you often can't look anyone in the eye because you feel they'll see all the things you're trying so hard to hide. And underneath it all is this desperate, aching thought: If anyone really knew me, they'd leave.

I didn't have words for it back then. I just knew I needed the feeling to stop. So I did the only thing I could think of: I hurt myself. I would dig my nails into my thighs or arms until the physical pain overtook the emotional one. I would watch as my skin reddened or even bruised. But I didn't want to die; I just wanted relief. I wanted someone to come and say, You don't have to hurt yourself to escape shame. But no one did, so I dealt with it on my own. That was how I survived.

Shame isolates. And even worse, shame lies. It tells you that you have to be alone in your pain, that comfort is for people who are better than you, and that your pain is proof you're unlovable.

But the truth is this: we were never meant to carry pain alone. We were always meant to be held and comforted, and to have someone return after we make a mistake and say, I see what happened. Let's make it right. I'm here now.

When multiple mistakes are made without the right repair,

the nervous system starts to reorganize around survival. Instead of saying to themselves, I made a mistake and someone helped me make it right, a child concludes Mistakes mean I lose love. And they eventually come to think My very presence must be the mistake.

Children are concrete thinkers. They can't imagine that a caregiver's rage, silence, or inconsistency might originate in that adult's wounds, so they assume it comes from themselves. And the body records every unsoothed moment, translating it into a warning: don't speak, don't need, don't trust. That's where shame is born.

But guilt is different. Healthy guilt can be sacred. It says, Something doesn't feel right. Let's look at it together. It allows for growth, reflection, responsibility, and repair.

Think about a moment when you were short with someone you love. Maybe you snapped at your partner, ignored a text, or rolled your eyes at your child. And afterward, something inside you whispered, That wasn't who I want to be. That's healthy guilt talking. It doesn't mean you're bad, only that you care and that something you did didn't align with who you want to be. Part of you longs to make things right.

Not all guilt is healthy, though. Trauma can leave us feeling guilty for things that were never wrong: having needs, setting boundaries, saying no, protecting ourselves, or surviving something we didn't cause. That kind of guilt doesn't guide us toward repair because there is nothing for us to repair. It asks us to take responsibility for pain that was never ours to carry.

Healthy guilt doesn't collapse you; it calls you back to connection. Shame, on the other hand, tells you that you are the bad thing, that you always ruin relationships and don't deserve forgiveness. It doesn't offer a path forward but just loops you in fear and self-abandonment. This is how healthy guilt liberates and shame traps.

Shame doesn't live only in childhood memories, though. It shows up in adulthood too: during meetings when you stay silent even though you have something to say, and in text messages you reread twenty times, afraid you've said too much. It pops up in parenting, in friendships, and in love. You find yourself constantly monitoring your tone and your needs. It's the fear that even your healing might be too much.

To begin healing, we must first let shame speak. Shame is the child at the back of the room with her head down, waiting to be punished again. But she doesn't need discipline. Instead, she needs someone to kneel down beside her, gently place a hand on her back, and say, You were never meant to go through this alone.

That's where healing begins: in presence and attunement, in letting that child be seen without fear and heard without shame. The child must ever so slowly be shown what it feels like to be met with kindness instead of blame.

There is no need for punishment or judgment. Healthy guilt should be accompanied by compassion. Compassion doesn't erase responsibility. It helps us stay present long enough to take it, make repair where possible, and choose differently the next time.

And when the guilt was never ours to carry, compassion helps us lay it down. It says, You were never the bad thing. You were just the child left without comfort, repair, or understanding. Let's grieve that together and learn how to offer what was missing. Let's come back home to truth.

Shame loops, but guilt liberates.

And the liberation isn't necessarily loud: it doesn't always come with fireworks or fanfare. Sometimes it feels like exhaling after years of holding your breath. It can be like hands unclenching and finally being able to rest. It comes when the part of you that learned to self-punish learns to self-soothe instead, the hurt is met with presence, and the storm is witnessed rather than silenced.

It comes when you whisper to the child inside, You don't have to hurt to be seen. You don't have to earn comfort; you deserve it no matter what. And you're allowed to heal.

This is what repair sounds like. It's a calm return to truth, to your breath, and to the self you never lost, only buried.

Shame kept you in the loop. But truth brings you home.

Sacred Pause

For the Ones Who Learned to Carry the Shame

Find a still, calm place, inside or around you. Let your shoulders drop and your jaw unclench. Let your belly be unguarded for a moment. Now close your eyes if that feels safe, and take a breath: the kind of breath that says, I'm still here and makes room for healing.

Think back to a time when shame overtook you. Maybe it was loud and sudden. Or perhaps it was quiet but constant, like background noise you didn't know how to turn off. Let yourself remember and witness that time. Notice what it felt like in your body: the heat, the aching, the hiding, or the scrambling to fix or shrink or disappear. The way your voice curled inward or your heart braced for the next blow, even when none came.

Now place a hand on your chest or your belly, wherever the pain still lingers. Breathe into that place like you're giving it things it never had: permission, safety, and presence.

You don't have to make it better. You just have to stay. Now say to that part of yourself: *You didn't deserve to go through that alone. You were not the bad thing. You were the one trying to survive what no one saw clearly enough to name.* Let this breath be for the child who thought the shame was her fault. Let it also be for the grown-up who still flinches whenever someone says, *We need to talk.* And let it be for every version of yourself that believed comfort was for someone else.

You're allowed to come home to yourself right now. You don't have to wait until you're healed. You can do it in this moment, just as you are: bruised, perhaps, but also beautiful and in the process of becoming your true self.

Let this be a sacred pause. Rather than an escape, see it as a return, a journey to the place inside you where shame has no authority. In this place, there is only the hushed voice of truth, whispering, *You were always worthy of being seen, and never meant to carry this alone.*

You are for...

You are for being seen without shame,
Held without earning it,
Loved without condition.

You are for hands that soothe,
Eyes that understand,
And voices that return to say, *You didn't deserve that.*

You are for the sacred work of returning,
Not to the pain,
But to the truth that was buried beneath it.

You are not the bad thing.

You are the brave one,
Still here, still reaching,
Still worthy of every soft place love was always meant to land.

Sacred Lesson from True:
Grief Follows Knowledge

I didn't expect grief to follow healing, but it does, every time. This happens because healing brings knowledge, and knowledge brings loss.

When I first met my True, the braver, kinder, wiser self buried beneath all the shame, I felt a sense of lightness and awe. I felt that I had finally come home. But I also felt something else: grief. A deep, aching grief came with the realization that no one had ever seen her, not my parents, not anyone else who was supposed to love me dearly, and not even myself.

My family had seen my fear, as well as my shutdowns, outbursts, and survival strategies. But they'd seen all this through their own wounds, through stories they hadn't healed, fears they'd never named, and beliefs that had never been mine to carry.

Sometimes they saw me as a threat; I was too loud, too emotional, and just too much for them. Other times they saw me as a reflection of their own failure, proof they hadn't done enough or hadn't done it "right." And sometimes, they placed me on a pedestal because I seemed like I was doing better, because I was surviving in ways they didn't know how to name.

For a long time, I mistook that pedestal for love. Being admired felt close enough to being known, especially when the alternative had so often been criticism, rejection, or shame. If someone saw me as strong, successful, or capable, I thought perhaps they were finally seeing me. But they were still seeing what I could do, not necessarily who I was.

Placing someone on a pedestal isn't love; it creates an obligation to perform. And if I'm on a pedestal, I'm lonely, because I'm not in a relationship. I'm being watched, not held, and admired, not known. There is no room on a pedestal to be confused, tired, needy, or wrong. The moment you become human, you risk disappointing the person who needed you to remain above them.

Pedestals don't make us partners; they create hierarchies where connection should be. One person becomes the savior, while the other is inevitably made invisible.

So yes, healing brought grief, because it showed me all the times I'd confused visibility with intimacy, achievement with acceptance, admiration with affection, and control with care. It showed me that some people who'd walked with me were only ever walking with a version of me that made them feel better, not a version that was true.

Sometimes, healing brings more loss, because you're finally whole enough to tell the truth. For example, the fact that they never really saw you, that they never really earned the right to be close, and that proximity isn't the same thing as intimacy.

And that hurts, because for a long time, their presence felt like love, and their attention felt like connection. But now you notice the difference: you see who couldn't hold your truth, only their own projections. You begin to understand that someone can know the details of your life without ever knowing your heart.

Grief follows knowledge, but honor does, too. Once I saw my True and met the version of me who didn't need to earn her worth, I also began to set her free.

I've learned to honor myself. I no longer confuse closeness with safety or betray my light just to be chosen. I've stopped accepting attention as a substitute for love. I've learned to set boundaries so that the people closest to me are the ones who protect my vulnerability at all times and at all costs.

That's what I'm for. I am not meant to be overlooked or idolized. Neither am I meant to be tolerated, envied, or used. I am for sacred, mutual, and fiercely protective love. I am for people who guard my gentleness like treasure. I am for spaces where my True gets to stay visible rather than needing to hide to keep the peace.

Grief follows knowledge. But so do truth and freedom.

Once you see yourself clearly, you stop whispering your worth to those who never leaned in to hear it. You stop shrinking to fit their comfort or dimming your light to preserve the peace. Instead, you begin to choose.

You choose presence over performance, and protection over pedestals. You choose the sacred few who meet your vulnerability with reverence and allow you to remain fully human.

Now you will remember that you were never meant to be admired from afar. You were always meant to be loved up close.

Sacred Pause

Let the Grief Be Holy

Take a breath. Place your hand on your chest. Feel the rise and fall of your body, the body that carried you through the times you were unseen and survived being misunderstood and misnamed. Let yourself mourn the moments people didn't see you and you felt obliged to hide parts of yourself just to stay connected.

It isn't weak to grieve what you missed. It's sacred. If you feel the need to cry or scream, please do so. If you need to sit in silence, do that. But do it as someone who finally sees clearly. You aren't grieving because you're lost but because you've finally come home to the truth, and that kind of grief is holy.

Let yourself be held now, by breath, light, and love.

You're not in hiding anymore.

You are for...

You are for sacred love, not pedestal performance.

You are for truth-tellers, light-holders, and safe witnesses.

You are for boundaries that protect your gentleness rather than punishing it.

You are for being seen fully, not just when you're easy to admire.

You are for choosing connection that honors your light.

You are for no longer begging to be chosen.

You are for resting in the truth: you were never too much, only too real for those who weren't ready.

Sacred Lesson from True:
You Are Allowed to Heal What Someone Else Refused to Repair

Some people will never repair what they broke or name what was lost. They'll never admit how deep the breaking went, or even that anything was broken at all. But that doesn't mean it wasn't real or can't be healed.

You're allowed to heal what someone else refused to repair, even if they deny what happened, have forgotten it, or say, "That was a long time ago."You don't have to carry their avoidance as your inheritance.

Some of us grew up in families where trauma was normal but repair was nowhere to be found. Apologies were absent, silence was louder than truth, and emotions were dismissed because survival took up all the space. Generations raised in survival mode don't always know what repair looks like because their parents never offered it. Their childhoods were marked by scarcity, not just of food or money, but also of gentleness, attunement, and emotional safety.

The message was usually, "You're fine. Toughen up, grow up, and get over it." So we did. We learned to suppress and hide things and to perform instead of connect. Sometimes the closest we got to repair was saying, "I'm sorry," just to stop the tension. We didn't say this because we truly understood, but simply because we were afraid. We thought maybe if we said the right words quickly enough, we could keep the love from leaving.

That was just survival, not repair. It was a fear response disguised as contrition. And when that becomes the pattern, we forget what real repair is supposed to feel like: safe, connected, and true.

A little over a year ago, I learned what it feels like to be on the other end, when someone you care about doesn't allow you to repair. An employee I truly respected left a note on her last day working for me, saying she had been angry with me for three years. She was going out on her own, and I admired her courage. But still, the idea of three years of unspoken anger stunned me and profoundly saddened me.

How could we have worked together, laughed together,

and shared space for so long without my realizing anything? I spiraled at first. I felt like I was sixteen again, being blamed for something I didn't even know about and couldn't fix. The shame came in fast, the way it always does when old wounds get reopened. But I let it come.

After a few weeks of sitting with this hurt, I asked myself, "Am I safe for people to come to?" That question cracked something open in me. The honest answer was sometimes yes, but sometimes no. I've had to work on that because safety isn't just a feeling. It is also a practice and an attitude.

Maybe she didn't feel safe because I hadn't created enough of a safe atmosphere. Or perhaps she hadn't done enough of her own work to speak hard truths when they mattered. It could have been both of these things, but I'll probably never know.

That's the thing about something breaking. There are layers to it, and not everyone is ready to peel them back. But the possibility of repair begins when one person chooses to stop the silence. It begins when we say, "That mattered. You mattered. And I want to make it right."

Repair isn't about being right but being real. Repair is about remembering that the relationship matters enough to address the problem honestly. It says, "This connection is worth pausing for, protecting, and tending. Your truth deserves a home inside something safe."

And repair doesn't erase the pain. It honors it and makes space for the hurt to be seen and held rather than buried or denied. Healing doesn't mean you have to invite everyone back in and reconcile with the people who harmed you. Some doors are meant to stay closed, and some boundaries are meant to be sacred.

You get to choose who's safe enough to witness your healing. Repair doesn't chase or beg. It offers an opportunity for restoration, whether that leads to reconnection or release. It offers conversation and compassion rather than blame, avoidance, or collapse.

You are allowed to learn the language your family never spoke and to write new endings for old wounds. Above all, you are allowed to build something whole, even if what you were handed was broken.

And sometimes, repair doesn't resemble reconnection. In some cases, it's just a soft release, a knowing that this person was meant to exit your life when they did. And that's okay. Closure doesn't always come through conversation. Sometimes it arrives through acceptance, through the peace that blooms when you stop chasing what will never come.

That too is repair: a sacred, self-given kind. It's the sort of repair that doesn't ask permission or wait for the other person to be ready. Instead, it rises from within once your heart finally whispers, "I don't need them to heal for me to be whole. I don't need them to see the pain for me to honor it. I don't need their apology to set myself free."

The most powerful repair is the kind you give yourself: the one that stitches back together what was torn without asking anyone else to hold the needle.

And most of all, you are allowed to offer your younger self the repair they never received, the tenderness they were denied, and the safety they only dreamed of. You can be the voice that says, "You didn't deserve what happened, and you don't have to carry it alone anymore."

You are allowed to rebuild what no one taught you to build. And you are allowed to call that sacred.

Sacred Pause

For the Ones Who Were Never Repaired

Take a breath: the kind that reaches all the way down to the place where silence used to live.

This pause is for the ones who tried, who reached out, who wrote a letter or asked for a conversation and were met with silence, denial, or blame. It's for the ones who never got the apology or heard the words they needed to, and the ones who had to stitch their healing together with thread they spun themselves.

It's for the ones holding grief in one hand and clarity in the other, who finally saw that the relationship they longed to repair was never built to hold them fully.

This pause is sacred. Rather than resignation or defeat, it is the holy calm that comes after you choose your own peace over someone else's patterns.

Let yourself feel what's ending. Let yourself honor what was lost.

And then, let yourself rise with what remains: your truth, your tenderness, and your right to rebuild in the company of those who are willing to meet you there.

Letting go doesn't mean you're broken.
It means you're whole enough to begin again.

You are for...

You are for repair that begins within.
For healing that doesn't wait for permission.
For honoring pain even when no one else sees it.

You are for gentle goodbyes that still hold love.
For brave boundaries that protect your light.
For letting go, not with bitterness, but with sacred clarity.

You are for safety that doesn't silence you.
For connection that sees you.
For relationships where truth is allowed to breathe.

You are for being the one who chooses to stop the cycle.
The one who feels it all and keeps loving anyway.
The one who says, This ends with me.

You are not here to carry the brokenness forever.
You are here to become the repair.

And you are still,
even now,
for love.

The kind that stays.
The kind that listens.
The kind that doesn't require you to disappear in order to belong.

The kind that meets your voice with softness,
your story with reverence,
your truth with a willingness to understand.

You are for repair that holds safety and connection.
Repair that looks you in the eye and says,

I see you. I hear you. I want to get this right.

You are for sacred healing,
where love is no longer earned through silence
but offered freely, just because you exist.

Sacred Theme Three

Boundaries, Repair, and Relationships

Sacred Theme Three:
Boundaries, Repair, and Relationships

Some of our deepest wounds were woven inside relationships, so it makes sense that healing must happen there too. We were taught things about love that weren't true, for example that love meant silence, connection required sacrifice, and saying "no" would cost us everything.

But True knows a different way. This theme is about honoring the sacred edges of your being and understanding that boundaries aren't walls to keep people out but bridges to connections built on truth. Repair isn't always about returning to a relationship. Sometimes, it's only about returning to yourself.

You're allowed to outgrow what used to fit. You have the right to speak the truth, even when it shakes things up. You have the freedom to say "no." And you'll still be lovable when you do.

These lessons will walk with you through the places where something broke and offer you the kind of repair you were always worthy of. Being perfect isn't necessary to deserve it; you deserve it simply because you're human and healing is your birthright.

- Intent Doesn't Negate Impact
- Boundaries Are Living Things
- Punishment Shames but Discipline Trains
- You Are Allowed to Have More (And Still Say "No")

Sacred Lesson from True:
Intent Doesn't Negate Impact

So many times in my life, trauma was excused, or even worse, erased. I was told, "It didn't happen that way" or that someone had just been doing the best they could. My mother told me she'd just wanted to be a good mom. But I never needed to hear what they had meant to do. I already knew they weren't good at parenting. What I needed was connection. I needed someone to help repair the mess, to honor the pit of trauma between us instead of pretending it wasn't there.

I needed them to approach gently, to take ownership and let me have my experience, because impact matters. Even when something wasn't intended to harm, it did. And when harm is done, healing can only begin with acknowledgment.

At the heart of complex trauma lies an unmet need for safety and connection. That's what gets passed down: not just pain, but the absence of what was needed most. And if no one names it or repairs it, the hurt gets inherited. It may be hushed and invisible, but it's very much alive.

We may not always intend harm, but once we know the impact we've caused, we're responsible for addressing it. This is our invitation to tend what was broken. We are accountable for what we choose to do next. And that's what I chose: to stop passing on what I wasn't meant for, and to stop excusing harm just because it wasn't intended.

But before the healing came, I just felt like a bad mom myself. All the time. Everything I did felt wrong. The only voices in my ear were those of my caregivers and my wounds. I knew what I didn't want to do with my kids, but I didn't yet know how to do things differently.

There were moments I felt angry. And because I'd been taught that anger was dangerous and rage was bad, I turned it on myself. I felt ashamed for feeling anything at all. And in that shame, I lost access to my intuition. I parented solely from a place of fear and a sense of urgency, but this only led to more silence and withdrawal, or at times more slammed doors and arguments I didn't know how to stop.

My children didn't want to tell me what was going on because I didn't feel safe to come to. And that's the part that wrecked me.

But my healing changed everything. It brought me and my children closer together. Although I hadn't magically become perfect, I was now present. When I learned to regulate my emotions, I gave them a mother who could hear hard things without falling apart. I gave them safety, not just in terms of what they were allowed to tell me, but also a safety their bodies could begin to trust.

I stopped needing to be seen as a good mom and started needing instead to be real, and realness opened the door to connection. It taught my kids that they could say whatever was true for them, even if it was hard for me to hear. That's what healing gave us.

But healing didn't erase my past mistakes or protect them from the things I still hadn't unlearned. There were things I'd done that had hurt them, and times I hadn't listened or had dismissed their feelings. In some situations, I hadn't been able to see past my own wounds to truly see them. Sometimes I'd made them carry things I hadn't yet set down, beliefs I'd never meant to pass on, but did.

And here's what I've learned: generational trauma confuses reflection. I once believed my children were reflections of me. So whenever they cried, or struggled, or pulled away, I took it personally. I would think, *What does this say about me? Am I failing?*

Yet my children don't exist to reflect me or confirm whether I am a good mother. They are their own radiant people, whole, sacred, and unique. But like all children, they absorb what surrounds them and internalize what's repeated. Their responses can reveal some of the impact of the beliefs, coping mechanisms, and patterns we've handed them, and sometimes that reflection can be hard to look at.

It seemed easier to try to fix them than to ask myself what their experiences were revealing about me. My natural response was to quote what I'd been told or to fall back on what the Bible said. I would cling to how I'd been raised instead of asking, Does this actually feel like love?

The realization that my kids were sometimes afraid to talk to me brought me to my knees. What I'd wanted most of all was to be safe for them, so it was difficult to learn that I sometimes wasn't. This had happened because I was still learning how to love myself and figuring out what love wasn't.

There are still days when I fall into shame and replay the moments I wish I could redo. Days I feel crushed by what I didn't know when they needed me to know it. But I'm learning to hold the grief without letting it bury the truth.

I came back, I got help, and I listened and changed. Now they tell me they love me and are proud of me, and that they feel safe.

But I still wish I could go back in time and talk to them the way True talks to me. I would sit beside them and hold their pain without rushing to fix it. I would say, *I see you. I hear you. You make sense.*

But while I can't change the past, I can do all those things now. I have finally learned what I was meant for all along. And I have stopped passing down what none of us were ever meant for.

A healing intention doesn't mean you'll never create a painful impact. It means you're willing to acknowledge that impact, remain present, and participate in repair. Things begin to change when you stop trying to be right or control others and instead learn how to be with them.

When you do this, the reflection starts to change and safety begins to grow. The pattern begins to break because someone finally chooses to love differently.

Sacred Pause

For the Ones Who Have Wondered If It's Too Late

If you're reading this with a heavy heart because you've yelled when you meant to listen, you've shut down when they needed you to stay open, or shame still whispers that you're a bad parent, pause here.

Breathe. This is not the end of your story.

You are allowed to grieve the past. But more importantly, you are allowed to change, and to love differently than you were taught. You don't have to fix the past to be a safe parent in the present. There's no need for you to have all the answers to start listening. You don't have to be perfect to become someone they can come to.

Start here. With breath, honesty, and presence. That's enough.

It's powerful and it's how the pattern ends.

You are for...

You are for repair.

For gentleness after silence.
For presence instead of perfection.
For hearing what was once dismissed,
and holding what was once too heavy.

You are for becoming the kind of parent
your child, and your inner child, can feel safe with.

You are for truth, tenderness, accountability, and change.

You are for healing the impact,
no matter the intent.

And you are for loving differently
so love can finally feel like love.

Sacred Lesson from True:
Boundaries Are Living Things

I used to think boundaries were a final destination, something you could set once and everything would get better. But healing has shown me that boundaries are actually living things. They grow with us, shifting as we gain greater insight. They ask us to listen, again and again, to the subtle voice inside us.

This year, as I've been writing about the most tender parts of my life, I've needed more space, especially from family. It isn't that I don't love them, but I've found that proximity sometimes keeps the wounds open. The temporary distance I've taken has given me breath. It's brought me the silence I needed so I could hear my own voice.

So when the Mother's Day group text came asking for a headcount, I felt the old panic rise. I wanted to lie, to say "yes" and then come down with the flu later. That would once have kept the peace. But I wouldn't have felt right about it, and peace that requires me to override my body isn't peace at all.

In my family of origin, "no" was never enough; you had to have a good excuse. And this meant we learned to lie, because we never felt safe telling the truth.

But I want something different now. I want to live in truth, even when it's misunderstood. So before replying to the group text, I paused to listen to what my body already knew: this wasn't something I wanted to do. And instead of apologizing or over-explaining, I simply said, "I won't be able to make it, but I'll be thinking of all of you."

That was it. I felt no guilt, and I made no dramatic exit. I just set a boundary that made me feel at peace. After all, boundaries aren't walls or punishments, and they're not just about saying "no."

Boundaries are sacred, and they're how we learn to stay with ourselves. They're holy ground where we reclaim the parts of us that were scattered by our efforts to simply survive. When we set boundaries, we stop abandoning our inner world for the sake of outer approval.

I've come to understand boundaries through my own TEMPS model, which has become a compass for recognizing what I need to protect:

T is for Time, because my time is not just a resource; it's a reflection of my values. I get to choose where it flows and what it fuels. I'm allowed to protect it from urgency, expectation, and being constantly accessible. My time is a sacred rhythm, not a debt that I owe.

E is for Emotion, because my feelings matter. I shouldn't have to shrink them or stretch them for anyone else's comfort. I also get to decide how much emotional energy I want to be around and how much I want to give. Not every storm is mine to stand in. Nor is every silence mine to fill.

M is for Material, because what I give or share, whether it's money, energy, labor, attention, or presence, should come from a place of fullness, not depletion. Generosity is beautiful, but not when it's extracted through guilt. I'm allowed to pause before pouring.

P is for Physical Space, because my body is my first home. I get to choose who enters it, who touches it, and what it needs to feel safe. I get to decide how much rest I need, what kind of environment nourishes me, and what I want to move toward or away from.

S is for Safety, Self, and Spirituality, because I am not here to betray myself to keep the peace. My inner world deserves protection. Peace is not a luxury, but a need. And my spiritual life is not negotiable. What makes me feel close to love, to True, to something sacred, is mine to honor.

Whenever any one of these is repeatedly overrun, depleted, or dismissed, I begin to lose connection with something sacred within me. And when I honor them, when I truly listen to what each part of me needs, I begin to rebuild trust within myself.

What I'm learning, gently and sacredly, is that boundaries are not barriers. They're offerings, living, breathing gifts I give myself so I can stay rooted in what's true. So I don't abandon myself trying to belong where I'm not meant to be.

And because boundaries are living things, they will continue to change as I do. What feels right today may not feel right tomorrow. They ask me to keep listening, to keep noticing, and to trust that I'm allowed to respond to what I need now.

They represent my own love returning to me, forming around me like a shelter of self-respect.

Sacred Pause

For the Boundary Beneath Your Breath

Take a slow, steady breath. Let it travel all the way in, past the place where you've been holding it.

And ask yourself gently: *Where have I been stretching too far, for too long? Where have I been shrinking so small that I've started to disappear? What part of me is whispering for space to exist, to breathe, or to feel without fixing?*

You don't need permission to protect your peace. You don't have to explain why your "no" matters. You don't owe anyone the version of you that always says "yes."

You're allowed to listen to your body, your breath, and your boundaries. You're allowed to change your mind. And you're allowed to choose yourself, even if no one claps for it.

Now place your hand over your heart, your belly, or anywhere that hurts. And say softly, like a promise: I am allowed to stay within what holds me well. *I am allowed to honor the sacred rhythm of my life, even when it moves me away from what once felt familiar.*

Let your body remember this:

boundaries are not rejection.

They're what enables reconnection, the threshold where self-abandonment ends and sacred self-respect begins.

You are for...

You are for sacred rhythms, not constant output.
For stillness without apology.
For choosing what nourishes you, even if others don't understand.

You are for honoring your time, your truth, and your tenderness.
For saying "no" without shame.
For leaving the door open only when it feels safe to do so.

You are for protecting your peace, not proving your worth.
For quiet exits that don't need justification.
For remembering that love can include space and still be love.

You are not too much.

You are not selfish for needing space.

You are sacred.
And your boundaries are the shape of that sacredness made visible.

You are for love that returns to you, from you,
soft, strong, and true.

Sacred Lesson from True: *Punishment Shames but Discipline Trains*

True taught me that punishment and discipline are not the same thing, unlike what many of us were raised to believe.

Punishment is rooted in shame and the desire to make someone pay. It can explode from frustration, coming from a place of fear, control, or emotional chaos. It says, "You've failed, and now you must pay." It's often doled out by an adult who doesn't know how to regulate their own emotions, let alone guide a child through a moment of struggle. So instead, the adult reacts with anger, threats, silence, hitting, shaming, or isolation. And the child learns: *When I get it wrong, love leaves. When I make a mistake, I lose connection.When I need help, I am punished.*

And over time, we stop trying or asking for help. We don't get to see that mistakes are just part of learning. Instead, we scan for signs of disapproval and brace for its impact. We become master performers, afraid to fall out of line and fearing that failure means rejection. Even in adulthood, we carry that terror, thinking *If I mess up, I'll be abandoned. If I struggle, I'll be shamed.*

Discipline is different. It's slow, intentional, and rooted in connection. It says, "You're struggling, and I'm here to help you learn." Discipline doesn't humiliate; it teaches. And it doesn't react; it responds. It's the consistent guidance that says, "I see you. I still love you. Let's figure this out together."

Unlike punishment, discipline teaches the body that correction can happen without the loss of safety or belonging. That's why those of us who were raised on punishment struggle so deeply with self-discipline. We think discipline means being harsh with ourselves, and that if we fail, we deserve to suffer. If we didn't get it right the first time, we must be broken.

So we punish ourselves with diets, restrictions, shame spirals, and perfectionism. We say, "I can't believe I did that again. I'll never get this right. I'll never be enough." We overwork ourselves to exhaustion and pick apart our bodies in the mirror. We rehearse conversations obsessively, trying to avoid criticism. We apologize for taking up space, needing rest, and having emotions. We parent ourselves with a voice that sounds eerily like the ones we once feared.

We forget that true discipline has grace, that it says, "Of course you didn't get it right the first time. You're learning." It's about the process rather than punishment. It's not all or nothing; it's try, adjust, and try again.

Those who were raised on punishment often have no map for this. They expect themselves to perform perfectly without ever having been guided gently. They believe discipline is about control, when it's really about care. And it's heartbreaking, because how can you follow a path you were never shown? How can you practice grace when all you've ever known is punishment?

This is what's difficult about reparenting: realizing what you missed while also learning to offer it to yourself now. Although it's not easy, we must grieve the absence and still choose presence, remembering that we have to create the map as we go along.

Perhaps the most painful thing is that we often pass that same pattern on to ourselves, again and again, punishing instead of nurturing, quitting instead of recalibrating, and shaming instead of gently course-correcting. We do this because we never saw discipline practiced with love.

But True shows us another way. She steps into the places where punishment once lived and gently whispers, "You were never meant to be treated that way." She sees the young part who flinched when the door slammed, who braced for the belt, the slap, or the silence. She sees the adult who now flinches at their own reflection, who speaks to themselves with the same cruelty they once endured. And she wraps them both in compassion.

True never raises her voice or demands anything. She doesn't force change through fear. Instead, she kneels down beside the trembling child within and says, "You were never bad. You were never broken. You needed guidance, safety, and care." She places a hand lightly on their chest, helping them breathe again. She rocks them gently, the way someone should have long ago.

And in that stillness, a new kind of learning begins, one

that says, "You don't have to earn tenderness. You were always worthy of kindness."

Then True turns to the grown-up self who tries so hard to get it all right, and she says, "You don't have to be perfect to be loved. You don't have to punish yourself to be good."

Discipline isn't about making someone suffer for what they've done. It's about care. Even when consequences are necessary, they can be offered without shame or the loss of connection. Discipline is the warm hand on your back that says, "Try again." It's the steady voice that reminds you, "You're still safe, even when you make mistakes."

True helps us slow down enough to hear our own hearts and realize that shame may teach us to hide and fear may teach us to comply, but neither one teaches us how to trust ourselves or create lasting change. That kind of learning requires safety, guidance, accountability, and love.

And so True shows us how to reparent ourselves in the moment, how to stop mid-spiral and say, "I'm learning." She teaches us how to choose curiosity over criticism and become a gentle guide to ourselves instead of our own harshest critic. When we sleep through our alarm, she whispers, "Let's try again tomorrow." When our body aches from overwork, she says, "Rest is not failure. It's wisdom." And when shame starts rising within us, she's there to guide us, saying, "Breathe. That was an old pattern. You don't have to punish yourself for repeating it. You are safe."

She helps us separate from the voices that once controlled us. And she brings us back home to the truth: discipline isn't punishment. It's protection, kind correction, and safe connection. Adjusting to these ideas may be a slow process. But this time, love gets to lead.

So if you find yourself spiraling, if your inner voice becomes harsh or the old scripts start playing again, pause for a moment. Touch your heart. And remember: you were never meant to be punished into wholeness. You were meant to be loved there.

Sacred Pause

For the Ones Who Are Learning Without Fear

Take a moment to notice where you are: not just the room around you, but where you are inside yourself.

You've made it through a lot, more than most people know. You weren't trained with tenderness but corrected with fear. You were expected to know things you were never taught and punished whenever you got it wrong.

That was never your fault. Let that truth settle for a moment. Allow yourself to feel how heavy it's been to carry that sense of aloneness. Recall how hard you've tried and how much of yourself you've turned against just to survive.

Now picture someone, maybe True or maybe someone else, who speaks to you with patience instead of pressure. Someone who stays by your side and doesn't shame you for struggling. Let yourself hear these words, even if just for a breath: *You are not bad.*

You were never meant to be punished into wholeness. You are worthy of learning in safety and receiving correction without cruelty. You deserve to be loved, even while you grow. And if part of you still flinches, fearing that you'll lose love if you mess up again, that part deserves the most tenderness of all.

This isn't just about getting it right. It's about being held in the moments you get it wrong, knowing you're not alone there anymore, and finding your way forward with love beside you.

You don't have to do it perfectly. Just stay with your breath, your heart, and the truth:

You are learning.
And you are loved as you learn.

You are for...

You are for learning gently, not performing perfectly.

You are for being guided, not shamed.

You are for being met with presence, even when you're struggling.

You are for nervous system safety, not fear-based control.

You are for being shown, again and again, that love doesn't leave when you mess up.
That your mistakes don't make you unworthy.
That your worth was never meant to depend on perfection.

You are for being held in your humanity.
For having space to try, to adjust, and to try again.

You are for the kind of care that teaches you slowly and steadily that you don't have to earn belonging.

You already belong.

Even when you forget.
Even when you fall short.
Even when you're learning how to love yourself through the things no one taught you to survive.

You are not a problem to fix.

You are a heart learning how to be safe in its own rhythm.

And you are worthy of being loved there.

Sacred Lesson from True:
You Are Allowed to Have More (And Still Say "No")

A certain kind of shame settles in when you start to have more than the people you came from. Note that this is definitely shame rather than guilt. The sense you get isn't, "I did something wrong," but, "I must be wrong for having more. I must be selfish for keeping any of it to myself."

This kind of shame doesn't come from nowhere; it's generational and systemic. It can become woven into family systems shaped by poverty and scarcity, where survival may depend on everyone sharing whatever they have. In such a system, having a little more means you're expected to give it away, and holding on to what you've earned can feel like betrayal.

I wasn't taught merely to be generous but to give even when I had nothing left. I watched women I loved give past their limits, over and over again. Their worth was tied to their sacrifice, their value measured by how much they endured without complaint. Boundaries weren't modeled for me. They only represented rejection. And the message was clear: if you have more, you owe more. If you have peace, you'd better make room in it for everyone else. If you say "no," you're breaking the family.

Part of the shame, if I'm being honest, came from remembering who I used to be. I remember looking at people who had more than me, for example, more money, more stability, or more choices, and not understanding why they couldn't just give. I couldn't see their limits because I was focused so intensely on my needs. And now that I'm on the other side, I carry that awareness too. It keeps me humble, reminding me that compassion can flow in both directions. But it doesn't mean I have to give myself, my energy, and everything I own away.

There was a time when calls from family came regularly, always with a request. And even before I answered, I felt it in my body. There was always a tightening in my chest, a swirl in my stomach, and the dread of knowing I was going to say "yes" when I didn't want to because I still hadn't addressed the shame of having more.

Then one day, my husband suggested something that changed everything. He said, "Let's give them one final gift. A one-time donation. And after that, let them know we're not the ones to call when money is needed." It was so simple and freeing. We gave from a place of clarity, not guilt. And for the first time, I set a boundary without apologizing for it.

I told them, "We're making this gift out of love, but moving forward, we won't be able to continue providing financial support. We trust you'll find the right next step." It was uncomfortable, but it was also honest. And that moment marked a turning point in my healing. I no longer tried to prove my goodness by giving myself away.

That same shame used to show up every single Thanksgiving. I'd begin preparing days in advance, shopping, chopping, cooking, and cleaning. By the time it was all done, my feet would ache, my body would be sore, and my mind would be spinning. I'd watch the pattern play out the same way every year: one or two people would do most of the work while the others watched football or slept in. Instead of saying how tired they were or asking whether the tradition still made sense, resentment would begin simmering beneath the surface. The unspoken questions were always there: Why isn't anyone helping? Must be nice to rest while I'm doing all this.

But here's the truth: none of us had ever actually agreed to this way of doing things. Someone, somewhere along the line, had decided that this was what Thanksgiving had to look like. And we all just kept repeating it, no matter the cost to our bodies or our peace.

Until one year when everything changed. About a month before Thanksgiving, my son called. I could hear the hesitation in his voice. He was trying to be respectful, but I could tell he was nervous. He said he and his wife weren't planning to come to the big family gathering that year. They didn't have kids, and they were both introverts. It felt like too much. Instead, they just wanted to spend the day together, quietly and intentionally.

And something in me softened when I heard that because what he had just done was let his True speak. That was courage.

And it gave me permission to ask myself a question I'd never dared to formulate: *What do I actually want?*

In trying to answer it, I realized I didn't want the chaos either. I didn't want to host and pretend it was all fine when it wasn't. I didn't want my home overrun with noise I didn't enjoy or expectations I never agreed to. I didn't want to keep performing the same version of myself that everyone else was used to.

So I said it out loud: "We're not doing Thanksgiving this year. We're not hosting or going to anyone else's place. We're staying home and honoring where we are right now."

And yes, there were whispers. Some people were hurt or thought we were breaking up the family. Others were angry that we weren't going to be on hand to help. I understood that the change might disappoint them, but I wasn't breaking the family. I was interrupting a cycle that had taught us to confuse obligation with love.

And that Thanksgiving was one of the best I've ever had. It was calm and connected. There was no tension or performance, no bracing for impact. Just a sense of peace that finally felt like mine.

This is what I know now: you are allowed to have more, whether it's rest, money, peace, or boundaries. You don't have to prove you're still "one of them" by abandoning yourself. You don't have to earn your right to rest, and you don't need to give to the point of depletion to be a good person. You don't have to answer every call that asks you to shrink.

I didn't owe anyone the version of me they preferred. Instead, I owed myself the version that could breathe. And for the first time, I experienced what it was like to choose peace without apology. That choice didn't make me selfish; it only made me free.

More than anything, I hope all my children always feel safe enough to tell me "no." They should feel free to say, "This doesn't work for me anymore," and to change their minds, even about things they once said "yes" to or traditions I hoped they'd carry on.

Love shouldn't require them to stay silent, or stuck, or small.

I want them to know that their truth is allowed to evolve and that nothing they say in honesty will ever cost them my love.

This is what healing looks like for me now: not just honoring my own boundaries, but creating a life in which my children's boundaries are respected, even when they are difficult for me to hear.

I owe them that.

Sacred Pause

For the Ones Learning That Enough Can Include You

Let yourself feel whatever rises within you as you read these words: the catch in your breath, the knot in your stomach, or the calm "yes" that whispers, *I know this story.*

You were taught to survive by disappearing and made to believe that love meant sacrifice. You grew up thinking that if you had more peace, more stability, or more ease, you should either hide it or hand it over. You learned this from an entire lineage of well-meaning women who only knew worth through what they gave.

This pause is for you. It's for the version of you who kept saying "yes" when your whole being ached to say "no." It's for the one who believed that generosity meant exhausting yourself, and that rest was a luxury someone else had to grant you. Let this moment soften what was hardened. Let it wrap around you like the gentlest warmth, like an heirloom quilt passed down not with a sense of scarcity, but with sacred reclamation.

You're not selfish for wanting to breathe or to change what no longer fits. You're not cruel for craving peace. This is not the end of love; it's the beginning of a love that includes you.

Let this pause be a place of truth. Let it remind you that boundaries don't break connection but create the conditions for it to be real. You can honor what came before without re-enacting what broke you. You can give and still belong to yourself.

And if the whispers come, those old voices questioning your goodness, may you meet them not with defense, but with clarity.

You're not abandoning the ones you love; you are just becoming the one who ends the inheritance of depletion. You are choosing a kind of peace that doesn't require performance and a kind of belonging that begins within: a family story that makes space for everyone's truth, including yours.

Let that truth rest in your bones now. Let it feel like coming home to what you've always known:

your healing matters,
wanting freedom is not asking too much,
and peace, chosen with love, is a sacred act of
remembrance and a radical act of becoming your truest self.

You are for...

You are for living unbound.
For holding sacred what fills you,
not just what empties you.

You are for saying "no" with love,
and "yes" without obligation.

You are for becoming the version of yourself
that no longer needs to prove her goodness
by bleeding out her joy.

You are for joy, too.
For quiet mornings and unshared holidays.
For laughter that doesn't have to be earned.

You are for breaking the unspoken rules
that told you your rest made others uncomfortable.

You are for rewriting what legacy means
not as endurance, but as truth.
Not as performance, but as presence.

You are for building a life that reflects your healing,
not your history.
A life where you no longer rehearse the role
they once handed you
but speak your lines from a new script
written in the language of enough.

You are for being the elder who says,
You don't owe me your exhaustion.
You don't have to dim yourself to stay in my light.
You can tell me "no," and I will still love you.

And you are for becoming that kind of elder for yourself, too.

The one who keeps watch at the gate of her own peace.

The one who blesses the boundary.

The one who rests without permission
because she finally knows she was always allowed.

Let this be your return,
not to obligation,
but to your own sacred rhythm.

Not to fear,
but to the deep-rooted safety of becoming whole.

Sacred Theme Four

Reclaiming Your Voice and Inner Wisdom

Sacred Theme Four:
Reclaiming Your Voice and Inner Wisdom

There is a knowing deep inside you that has never left. It may have been silenced, questioned, or buried beneath years of survival, but it's always been there, waiting, listening, and whispering the truth in quiet moments.

This theme is about coming back to that inner wisdom, the one that once said, "This isn't okay," and wondered, "What if there's more?" It's time to reconnect with this wisdom that asked questions long before anyone was ready to answer them.

When we reclaim our voice, we also reclaim our power. And when we trust ourselves, we begin to come home to who we are. These lessons will help you remember what has always been yours: your intuition, your insight, and your sacred right to trust what you know, question what you don't, and say, "I know what I need."

Sacred Lesson from True: *"I Don't Know" Is a Sacred Place to Begin*

When I was little, I wasn't allowed to say, "I don't know."That answer wasn't safe because, to my parents, it meant I wasn't paying attention or was being disrespectful. It somehow signaled that I was lazy, defiant, or dumb.

So I stopped saying it and learned to guess. I tried to fake it and offer the "right" answer before anyone could see through me. Sometimes I lied, but I did this only to survive. I didn't really want to be dishonest; I was only afraid.

Today, I remind my clients all the time that children often lie when they don't feel safe telling the truth. Often, we don't lie because we want to be dishonest. We lie because somewhere deep in our bodies, we learned that uncertainty wasn't allowed and that curiosity would get us hurt. Confusion can feel like something dangerous.

And so, instead of learning to wonder, I learned to watch. Rather than asking questions, I would scan the room for signs of danger. I didn't get to be a seeker but, out of necessity, became a sensor, tuned into every nuance of tone or gesture. In my world, knowing what to say wasn't about learning but about staying safe.

This is what trauma taught me: I had to have the answer, I had to get it right, and I could not disappoint. If I didn't know something, I had better pretend I did.

So I abandoned the part of me that was allowed to not know. I no longer thought about exploring things or following the spark of a question until it caught fire with insight. I had to leave these things behind because survival meant replacing curiosity with hypervigilance. I needed to watch for what was wanted before I even knew what I wanted myself. It was essential to always be two steps ahead if I wanted to stay clear of someone else's anger.

Even now, there are moments when the panic returns. If someone asks me a question I can't answer, my chest tightens, my mind floods, and a thousand parts scramble to fill in the silence. Even when I trust the person, my body remembers what it once cost me to get it wrong.

But the more I've healed, the more I've come to understand this sacred truth: "I don't know" isn't failure but a beginning.

Someone once told me, "'I don't know' is just a missing data point." And this changed everything for me. I realized that "I don't know" isn't emptiness but openness, a sign of potential. Admitting we don't know something is the start of discovery. It allows us to follow our own questions, in our own time, toward what's true.

True taught me that I'm allowed to pause and wonder, and to be curious without facing consequences. I have the right to ask questions, to not know everything, and to make space for new knowledge to arrive.

When we create enough safety, both internally and externally, we can stop performing in exchange for protection. We no longer have to pretend we're sure about something when we're secretly scared. We start trusting that not knowing something isn't dangerous but a doorway.

Now, when I say, "I don't know," fear may still rise, but it no longer gets to decide what happens next. I remember that not knowing means I'm rooted enough to pause, open enough to learn, and vulnerable enough to be surprised.

Wisdom, after all, doesn't come from having all the answers. It comes from being willing to remain present with the questions.

Sometimes the most sacred thing we can say is, "I don't know yet. But I'm here, I'm listening, and I'm willing to find out." Healing begins when we stop fearing the question and finally give ourselves permission to begin from the sacred place of not knowing.

Sacred Pause

For Every Time You Were Told You Should Already Know

Close your eyes. Place a gentle hand over your heart or your belly, wherever it feels safe to land. Take a slow breath in… and then let it out without rushing.

Let this truth settle in: You do not have to know everything to be worthy of love. You do not have to get it right to be safe here. You are allowed to ask, to pause, and to wonder.

Notice the space that opens up when you say the words "I don't know." Can you feel the relief of that? Let your body begin to soften, like it's unlearning a rule it never agreed to. Allow your breath to be an invitation to stay curious. See the silence as something sacred. And if an old part of you still panics, still wants to hurry, prove, or pretend, simply whisper back with love:

You don't have to know right now.
We are safe enough to begin again.

You are for...

You are for wonder.

For the spark that lights when a question arises.
For the sacred pause before an answer comes.

You are for learning, unfolding, and changing your mind.

For asking again.
For beginning again.
For not knowing and still being deeply, completely enough.

You are for sacred curiosity.

You are for the questions that lead you home.

You are for freedom that does not require performance.

You are for every truth still waiting to be discovered, especially the ones that belong to you.

Sacred Lesson from True:
I Had to Heal to See Them

I didn't grow up with a model for healthy parenting, and I didn't take a single parenting class until my daughter was fifteen. By then, we had already walked through fire.

From thirteen to fifteen, we struggled, sometimes quite a lot. She was finding her voice, and I was still trying to find mine. I was overwhelmed by her intensity, confused by her behavior, and constantly triggered. But beneath all of that, the truth was that I didn't know how to see her past my own wounds, and she didn't know how to trust me through hers.

One day, in the middle of one of our worst arguments, she looked at me and said, "I hate you!" It felt like a physical blow, not just because of what she'd said, but because I never would've dared say that to my own mother. I may have felt it growing up and may have thought it many times, but the words never crossed my lips. In my family, that kind of truth wasn't allowed. Fear kept it sealed inside because saying it would have resulted in violence.

But she said it out loud. And as much as it hurt, I knew in that moment that I wasn't going to hit her. I wasn't going to repeat what had been done to me. Even if I didn't know what to do yet, I already knew what I was determined not to do. I also knew that we needed help.

So I took her to therapy through her school. Things didn't change overnight, but something began to shift in me. I started sharing pieces of my own story in that therapist's office. And for the first time, I started to feel a tiny thread of compassion for myself, both for what I'd been through and for what I was still carrying.

It helped for a little while. But honestly, it still felt like nothing I did was good enough. I was pouring all my energy into her and still falling short. And the messages I was getting from my own family were brutal: "She just needs her ass beat," "You're too soft," and "Be tougher. Be louder. Be scarier."

But that wasn't the kind of mother I wanted to be. I didn't want to hurt her like I'd been hurt myself. I just didn't know how to do it differently yet.

Ironically, the real breakthrough didn't come from those therapy sessions but from my work. I was employed by a psychiatric hospital and worked in the children's unit. Some of the children returned to the hospital so often that staff referred to them as "frequent flyers." The team needed a parenting curriculum, and somehow, that task landed on my desk.

I found a program called *Parenting with Love and Logic* by Jim and Charles Fay. And I soaked it in like oxygen. I read every word of the accompanying book and watched every video again and again. I wanted to understand the material well enough to teach it, but my passion for it quickly became personal. I was truly excited by what I was learning for myself for the very first time.

I finally had a model, vocabulary, and tools to help me understand parenting. And slowly, miraculously, my parenting started to change. As this happened, my relationship with my daughter improved. I began to learn how to regulate my emotions and offer choices with dignity. I saw how I could connect without controlling and stay consistent without becoming punitive.

One key thing that no one had ever told me was that, as the parent, I had to be willing to do ninety percent of the work. And I had to let go of the hope that she'd meet me with the other ten because I was the adult, the one responsible for breaking the cycle. The most sacred repair I could offer was to see her clearly, not through my fear or my shame, but through the eyes of someone who was learning how to love without using fear or pain as tools.

The more I healed, the more I could see my kids for who they truly were. I no longer viewed them as extensions of myself or evidence of my success or failure. I also stopped looking at them as problems to fix. Instead, I saw them as whole, complex, beautiful beings with their own lives to live.

That healing showed up in big and small ways. But one of the most unforgettable moments was dancing with my son at his wedding. The second our hands touched, I began to cry. And it wasn't any quiet kind of crying. I was sobbing. For the first time, I felt present. I had finally healed enough to really see him.

There was grief in those tears, sorrow over what I'd missed and the years that seemed like a blur. I felt sadness for all the ways trauma had kept me distracted, detached, or reactive. But that grief didn't steal the moment or swallow my joy because I was there. I was in my body, dancing with my son. And it was beautiful.

This is what I know now: you don't heal only for your children; you also heal so you can see them. Healing helps you react less from your wounds and make more room for connection. It lets you honor their unfolding rather than trying to manage it.

Even if you didn't know how to show up at the beginning, there may still be an opportunity to begin again. There may still be time to look into your children's eyes and say, "I see you now. I'm learning. I'm here. And I won't stop trying." As long as there is an opportunity to begin differently, there is still time to build safety where there used to be tension, create gentleness where there was once harshness, and make new memories that don't have to pass through pain first.

There may still be time to hold their stories with open hands instead of gripping them with fear. You can welcome their truth, even when it stretches you, and let them be fully themselves without needing to shape them into a version that fits your unhealed places.

And no, I can't rewrite the years that trauma stole. But I can be here now, with my heart open. I can choose presence over perfection. I can love my kids without losing myself. And I can teach them, through my own becoming, that we are never beyond the possibility of learning how to love each other better.

Sacred Pause

For The Ones Who Are Still Learning

Take a breath. Let it be soft. Let it be yours.

You're not too late. You're allowed to grieve what you didn't know. You can forgive yourself now for parenting in survival. There's nothing stopping you from starting again, even if the beginning is messy. You don't have to be perfect to be present. You don't have to have all the answers to offer love. You just have to stay.

Now place your hand on your heart or over your belly, where so much truth is stored. Say gently to yourself: I can learn a new way. I can love without fear. I can see them now. And I can stay.

Let that truth rise inside you. You are healing the story, just by showing up differently.

You are for...

You are for seeing with healing eyes.

You are for pausing before reacting.
For choosing presence over patterns.
For becoming the parent you never had.

You are for seeing the ones you love, not through fear, but through the clarity that healing brings.

You are for honoring their journey, even when it doesn't mirror your own.
For saying, I see you. I'm still learning. I'm not leaving.

You are for repair.

You are for gentleness.

You are for love that doesn't need to control in order to connect.

You are for choosing again, this time, with open eyes.

Sacred Lesson from True:
You Don't Have to Climb Every Rope

For a long time, I believed healing had an endpoint. I pictured myself climbing a long rope, hand over hand, through grief and grit, just trying to reach the top and ring the bell. Then I would finally be able to say, *I did it. I'm healed. I'm done.*

But one day, a therapist told me, "Melanie, you're not in a room with one rope. You're in a gym full of them. There are hundreds of ropes, each with its own bell. And you're trying to climb them all." Once she put it like that, I really got it. It was true; I was climbing every rope I could find, past, present, future, trying to get it right, trying to get free.

But healing isn't about reaching the top. It's not about bells or badges or being finished. It's about learning when to climb and when to come down, taking the time to rest when you need to and letting someone else hold the rope. Sometimes, we need to stay grounded in the now instead of climbing for proof.

At one point, I was still going to therapy intensives twice a year. I thought I was healing the past. But then my therapist said something that changed my perspective. "You're not just healing old wounds," she told me. "You're also trying to survive what's still happening." That was the moment I realized I didn't need to go deeper. Instead, I needed to get clearer. It was time to set boundaries and stop merging with other people's pain. I needed to figure out who I was apart from everyone else's chaos.

And that hasn't been easy, because the truth is, I had a clearer picture of what I feared than of what I wanted. Even now, I still sometimes get overtaken by shame. I still get pulled into old stories, especially when I hear that someone's been gossiping about me. It can make me feel twelve years old again, bracing for impact. But now, I have the words I need to address it: "I don't want to hear gossip about me. If someone needs to talk to me, they can come talk to me."

I've learned that gossip rarely gives me the clarity I'm looking for. Whatever truth, misunderstanding, or hurt may be underneath it cannot be resolved through conversations that do not include me. I am for clarity. I am for sitting at the table, face to face, and figuring it out together. I've worked hard to become someone people can approach, but I've also had to accept that being safe doesn't mean allowing unsafe behavior. Safety works both ways, and gossip is not a substitute for honesty.

And it wasn't just about how others treated me. I had to look at the ways I'd been treating myself, too. There's a part of me shaped by people-pleasing that still wants to over-give, over-function, and make everything okay for everyone. For a long time, I convinced myself that this behavior was an expression of compassion or love.

But one day, my therapist told me something I didn't want to hear: "People-pleasing is actually selfish." I wanted to fire her and look for someone else.

"Selfish?" I shouted back. "You mean selfless! I thought I was being selfless. Isn't that what I'm supposed to do, make other people happy?"

She smiled at me. "No," she continued gently. "It's selfish because you abandon the part of you that's true and authentic, and you hand the other person a lie. You tell them it's okay when it's not. You make them believe you're fine with something you're silently resenting. And then you blame them for not knowing it was too much."

That hit like lightning. It was so true! And underneath it, I began to see an even deeper reality. People-pleasing doesn't come from a place of kindness alone. Much of mine came from a lack of safety. Beneath it was the belief, *If you're not okay, I won't be okay. And I can't connect with you until you're okay.*

I realized I'd learned to abandon myself in order to stay close to others. I'd mistaken attachment for connection and confused keeping the peace with keeping myself. And because I'd never felt safe enough to say what I really wanted, because I hadn't known I was allowed to have needs, I'd developed what another therapist once called "need shock." This happens when you have a need, but you don't know what it is, you don't know how to ask for it, and your whole nervous system floods. It's disorienting and loud inside when this happens. And just existing feels like failure.

But I've learned that when I feel that panic set in, I don't need to fix it right away. I just need to pause and breathe. I just have to give myself the space for it to move through. It always does; it just needs time and some compassion. And, perhaps most importantly, a witness.

Being able to name it aloud to my husband, a close friend, or in therapy, saying, I'm feeling shame instead of hiding it, helps me move through it. Shame keeps us trapped in the belief that we are bad. But when we bring this feeling out into the light, when someone sees us and still stays, we can begin separating who we are from what happened. If we caused harm, we can move toward responsibility and repair. If the shame was never ours, we can begin putting it down.

Part of this healing process was creating new structures, tools that could help me name what was safe and what wasn't. I developed my own tool that I call the Standard of Respect. It's made up of what I personally feel in my body to be true, kind, and safe rather than what others think is acceptable.

I even use this with my therapy clients now. I invite them to take a piece of paper and draw a line across the middle. On that line, they write "Standard of Respect." Below the line, we list behaviors that feel harmful or unsafe, things like yelling, name-calling, forcing others to walk on eggshells, manipulation, and emotional withdrawal. Then we explore how those behaviors make them feel: scared, small, alone, helpless, or bad. And we ask, What do those things make you believe about yourself?

Then we go above the line and name the things that feel good: the people who say kind words that make us smile, the relationships that feel gentle, open, and warm. We explore how those things land in the body and what they help us believe: that we're safe, we're valued, and we're allowed to be ourselves.

Often, that paper shows us something hard but honest. Sometimes the people we care about engage in behaviors that leave us feeling hurt, unseen, unsafe, or disconnected from ourselves. Sometimes it's not a person at all. It's a commitment, an expectation, a role we've outgrown, or a responsibility we're carrying that no longer fits. Once we see what consistently costs us peace, energy, or capacity, we can't unsee it. And from that new clarity, new choices can begin. Clarity like this doesn't stay on paper. It starts showing up in your calendar, your energy, and your capacity.

I had to take a long, honest look at what I was carrying. And I began putting some of it down: not just obligations I didn't want, but things I thought I wanted, too. This included ideas and opportunities that once seemed right but didn't leave space for what mattered most.

Writing this book has required more emotional space than I expected. And with that space came waves of shame. After all, it's not easy unfolding all this trauma and then turning around to hold someone else's. Pouring from a place you're still trying to fill comes with challenges. But I'm learning that making space for my healing isn't selfish. It's sacred.

And in the quiet, I began to notice the whispers I used to ignore and the places where the hurt still lived. Those tender places still need tending, because they prevent me from seeing clearly. When I don't slow down to tend them, I risk reacting to a memory instead of responding to what's real.

Running a group private practice has been one of the biggest mirrors of my life. I've learned what I love, what I dread, what I thrive in, and where I still struggle. And for a long time, the parts I didn't do well made me feel unworthy, as if I had to be good at everything, all the time.

Trauma had taught me I had to survive alone, but healing has shown me I should let others in. So I built a support system. I found people who shine where I stumble. Healing isn't about perfection, but permission. When you heal, you learn to ask for help, to be okay with leading imperfectly, and to build something sacred with others.

But eventually, I had to face a harder truth. Support could not make the role right for me once it no longer fit. Closing the group practice forced me to put down one of the heaviest ropes I had ever carried. It wasn't a rope I had failed to climb. It was a role that had taught me what it came to teach me. Releasing it did not erase what I had built or mean that none of it mattered. It meant I was finally listening to what my life was asking of me now.

Still, it's easy to glance sideways and feel the sting of what I call "not-enoughness." I've had to stop comparing myself with others, to quit looking around me and measuring my work against someone else's wins. Thanks to Brené Brown, I finally understood that what I was feeling was envy. It was an envy of things I longed for but didn't have. And instead of honoring that longing, I'd been using it as a weapon against myself.

But healing has taught me to come back to my own gifts, to what I do well, and to the truth that when my eyes are busy watching what everyone else is doing, I may be scanning the room for safety and asking myself, *Am I enough?* And the answer now is *Yes, I am.*

I don't have to keep climbing someone else's rope to prove the worth of my own life. I can let another person's success reveal something I want without using it as evidence that I have failed.

I've even had to relearn what it means to be sick. Emotional regulation takes energy, and complex trauma means we often use more energy than most just to stay balanced, just to be okay. So when a virus or flu hits, it draws from the same well we use to stay emotionally grounded. And after the fever fades or the cough clears, I've noticed I often still feel foggy, low, and off-center. That's biology; that's my body saying, *Please don't rush me. I need more time.*

But trauma tells us: *Get up! Shake it off! You're inconveniencing people.* So we forget how to recover. Healing reminds us that we aren't an inconvenience but a miracle, and miracles need rest too.

This work, this unraveling, remembering, and repairing, is a sacred return, not a race. When we heal, we come back to who we were before the world ever asked us to be smaller. We return to the truth beneath the tangle and the hidden light that never left.

There's no final bell to ring, no single rope that means you've made it. But if you're here, reading this, then you've already made one of the bravest climbs of all. You've chosen to stay, to keep going, and to come back to yourself.

The framework that helped me walk this path dwells beneath every chapter of this book. It isn't something you have to master; it's something you can gently live. If you're curious to learn more, there's more to come. There are ways to explore it gently, with others, or by yourself in your own way.

But for now, just enjoy this breath. And remember that you don't have to climb every rope. You only have to come home.

Sacred Pause

You Don't Have to Climb Today

Before you reach for another rope, try to prove you're okay, or scan the room to see who's doing it better, pause for a moment.

Place a hand on your chest. Let yourself feel the weight of your own presence. Don't think about your performance or your progress. Just your presence.

Breathe here. You've done so much to get to this moment. You've unpacked old beliefs. You've rewritten unhelpful patterns, chosen boundaries, and told the truth, even when it shook things up. You don't have to keep climbing all the time. You can rest. You can soften into the knowing that healing isn't earned through exhaustion. It's received through presence.

Ask yourself gently: *What part of me still believes I have to do more to be enough? What would it feel like to let that part rest today?*

You're not behind or failing. You're returning. And every return is sacred.

You are for...

You are for tenderness that tells the truth.

You are for boundaries born of love, not fear.

You are for pausing without guilt, and resting without explanation.

You are for saying what you need, even if your voice shakes.
Even if no one taught you how.

You are for remembering that connection doesn't require self-abandonment.

You are for walking away from what lives beneath your line,
and choosing again what lifts you back into your light.

You are for the breath that returns after the flood.
The truth that holds after the shame.
The safety that grows from within, not from approval.

You are for becoming, not a better version of who they expected,
but the real version of who you've always been.

You are for healing in your own time.
For love that doesn't leave.
For wholeness that was never actually lost.

And most of all,
you are for rising gently from the place you've come home to,
not to strive,
but to move with grace
in the rhythm of your sacred belonging.

Sacred Theme Five

Returning to the Body and Naming the Attachments

Sacred Theme Five:
Returning to the Body and Naming the Attachments

The body can hold on to things that the mind has had to push away. Long after the moment has passed, the body may still remember what was felt, what was feared, and what was never allowed to be expressed. And sometimes, the ways we tried to survive that pain became attachments we mistook for comfort. The following lessons are about returning to the body with gentleness, understanding what once protected us, and reclaiming what's been true all along.

This theme invites you to notice the knots you carry, the beliefs they created, and the power you now have to release them. It invites you to name your needs without shame and to feel your light rise in spaces where it used to hide. Survival does not have to be the end of your story. You're learning how to live.

- Body Shame to Body True
- You're Not Just Addicted, You're Also Attached
- From Knots to Warriors

Sacred Lesson from True:
Body Shame to Body True

There's a kind of shame that doesn't whisper. It lives inside your body like a warning, but it doesn't signal any danger outside of you. Instead, it warns you that you are the danger, telling you that your shape, your skin, your softness, your stretch marks, and your appetite need to be managed, hidden, or punished.

Body shame doesn't always arrive when others look at you. Sometimes, it sets in before you even leave the house. It can come when you're alone before the mirror, when you're trying on clothes, when you're remembering something someone said years ago, or when you're bracing for judgment that might never come because you've already judged yourself.

This kind of shame lives in the way we see ourselves. It makes us suck in our stomachs or calculate calories as a measure of our worth instead of considering what our bodies need. It drives us to dismiss the good things our bodies do because we've been taught to measure their worth by how they look.

I can't count how many shopping trips I went on hoping to feel beautiful but walked out with shame burning inside my soul. I'd go in for jeans, a dress, or a maybe-this-time piece. But I'd usually leave with only a purse or a pair of shoes because those always fit. Those things never called my body a problem. If I couldn't find something to wear, at least I could carry something that didn't make me feel like a failure.

As a result, I have so many purses and so many shoes, all of them little trophies of defeat. They're proof that I tried and still wanted to feel good, even if the dressing room mirror didn't let me.

Over time, I stopped expecting clothes to fit and started expecting shame instead. I'd stand in front of the mirror, holding my breath, not because the clothes were too tight, but because I was too much, too big, and too wrong. And even though I knew better intellectually, my body didn't. My body knew only that fitting rooms were dangerous and mirrors could hurt me. I felt that wanting to look good was somehow selfish or foolish when I should have just been grateful I had a body at all.

No one ever taught me that my body was good or that it was holy. I didn't receive this message at home, at church, or at school. Instead, I heard, "Cover up," "Watch what you eat," and "No one wants a girl who lets herself go." And if I ever dared to feel beautiful, that was pride. It was also dangerous because it meant I was asking for attention.

So I turned that beauty inward, folded it up, hid it, and tried to be invisible. I lost years to that war: years of not dancing, not swimming, dodging cameras, and turning down dates and invitations. It wasn't that I didn't want to take part; I just didn't want to be seen.

Shame became my second skin, a tight layer I couldn't shed. And I thought if I could just fix myself, just lose the weight, and just find the right lotion, the right angle, or the right version of me, then I'd be worthy of showing up. Then I'd get to belong. But I never got there because changing my body never healed the shame. That healing had to begin in my relationship with my body.

I've had to practice looking in the mirror again. For years, avoiding it was one of the ways I survived. Seeing myself had always meant seeing everything I'd been taught to hate. And shame didn't leave when I grew up; it grew up with me. It followed me into adulthood with the same cruel voice, echoing every comment and comparison.

Shame even followed me into compliments. If someone said, "You look beautiful," I would flinch inside and dismiss it. I couldn't believe them or receive it. When you've spent years believing you're unworthy, kindness often feels like a trick. It would only make me uncomfortable, and I'd always want to disappear. Even praise unrelated to my appearance would feel like a spotlight I didn't deserve.

My body was constantly pointed out for being different, even when it was healthy, even when it was strong. And now, I look back at old photos from times in my life when people had called me fat, and I want to scream: *What were you thinking? How could you have called that beautiful girl fat?* She was radiant. She was growing. She was becoming. And all she needed was someone to tell her, "You don't need to earn love by erasing yourself. You're already worthy."

But then True came. She didn't shame me for the shame. Instead, she honored my experiences and whispered to me, "You were never meant to be at war with yourself. Your body is not a battlefield. It's your home. You weren't made to disappear but to belong in your own skin."

She didn't ask me to love my body overnight. She simply asked me to return to it, one breath at a time, and to stop punishing it and measuring it against what was never real. True asked me to begin again with wonder.

My body is made for movement and rest, for tears and touch and tenderness. It isn't a project, it doesn't require apologies, and it isn't too much. It's mine. It's me. And the more I listened to True, the more I wanted to care for this body out of honor and love.

Now I believe that bodies are for being, not performing. They're for feeling, not flattening, and for celebrating, not comparing. And if someone sees only your body, they're not seeing your soul. They're not seeing all of you.

True reminds me daily, "Your body wasn't created to be viewed. It was created to be lived in." And this body, this sacred, storied body, belongs to me, not to shame, culture, or the voice that says, *Be smaller to be safe.* My body is mine. And I am slowly, bravely, coming home to myself.

Sacred Pause

Come Home to Your Body

Take a moment. Breathe in through your nose, slowly and fully. Let your breath touch every part of you that's been silenced by shame: all the places you've squeezed, judged, and tried to hide.

As you exhale, try to soften. Soften your belly, your shoulders, and the old story. You don't have to earn your way back into your body. You don't have to fix it or shrink it, sculpt it, or apologize for it. You are allowed to live in it, right now, as it is.

Place your hand over your heart or wherever you feel the most disconnection. Let this be your invitation: You are welcome here. You are safe here. And you are whole, even in the places that still ache.

This isn't about loving every inch every second. This is only about beginning again and returning. This is about coming home.

You are for...

You are for the truth of your body.

You are for living, not being looked at.

You are for feeling, not fixing.

You are for comfort, joy, and movement that feels like freedom.

You are for softness and strength and sacred shape.

You are for breath, rest, hunger, and delight.

You are for mirrors that bless, not betray.

You are for photos that capture your glow, not your shame.

You are for belonging, to yourself, before anyone else.

You are for being seen, without being reduced.

You are for reclaiming the voice that shame tried to erase.

You are for undoing the war.

You are for peace.

You are for presence.

You are for you.

Sacred Lesson from True:
You're Not Just Addicted, You're Also Attached

We talk about addiction like it's a weakness or the absence of willpower. We frame it as something broken that just needs to be fixed. But True taught me something different.

Sometimes, what we call addiction is also attachment in disguise. When you grow up in trauma, attachment becomes survival, even if what you're attached to hurts you and the only thing that ever stays is the thing that numbs you.

Addiction and compulsive patterns can take many forms. Substances like alcohol or drugs are what people usually think of, but we can also become attached to people, relationships, jobs, patterns, habits, or ways of thinking. Anything that serves as a cushion against your pain and offers comfort or the illusion of control can become difficult to let go of. That includes overworking and people-pleasing.

These things don't really offer connection. They're tethers, barbed-wire ropes that wrap around your wounds and say, *You may bleed, but at least you're not alone.* And that's why addictions are so hard to let go. Connection isn't just a want; it's a need. Your body needs it and reaches for it. And if you've never experienced safe, steady love, your body may attach to whatever makes you feel less alone, even if it's hurting you.

Over time, the addiction can become the attachment. And that attachment can feel like the only thing you have left. This was one of the hardest truths for me to face. Throughout my healing, I came to realize that what I thought was connection was actually just attachment. And some of those attachments weren't even that. They were like spaghetti, tangled and messy, with untraceable origins. They looked like love on the surface, but underneath, they were rooted in fear, obligation, or a familiarity that I mistook for safety.

And with that realization came grief. So much grief. It changed the dynamics of those relationships and altered the access I could allow. It affected what I was willing to carry. I finally understood that real connection is rooted in safety. And that's what makes it so different from attachment. Safety is the soil where trust grows. Without it, all we have are twisted roots and thorns.

I've had to make hard choices. Some involved relationships. Others involved roles I had outgrown, responsibilities that were no longer mine to carry, and expectations that kept me trapped in old patterns. Protecting my healing required me to recognize that not everyone has earned the right to my vulnerabilities and that connection does not require unlimited access. Some choices brought grief. Others brought relief. Most brought both.

I had to learn that boundaries aren't a betrayal of others but a way of protecting ourselves. They allow clarity, and they are sacred.

Some attachments show up as behaviors, as battles we've faced or still face from time to time. They can be patterns such as people-pleasing, over-functioning, perfectionism, rescuing others, avoiding conflict, or reaching for familiar comfort when life feels uncertain. They often show up like old companions in moments when connection feels far away.

Some of those patterns still knock on my door, whispering in my hardest moments, "This will help. This will soothe you. This will get you through." And sometimes, I listen. This doesn't mean that I've failed, only that I'm still healing. We must remember that healing doesn't follow a straight line. Recovery usually zigzags as we learn and practice new patterns. It may take twists and turns. It's a slow rebuilding of trust with ourselves, one moment at a time.

I'm still learning how to reach for presence instead of pain. I'm still teaching my body that it's allowed to rest, that comfort doesn't have to come with shame, and that love doesn't have to hurt.

Not all comfort heals. Some comfort harms. And sometimes, healing means taking bolt cutters to the barbed wire to break through to truth. We need to say, *I'm worth more than this pain. I'm allowed to want more than survival. I'm ready for something real.*

Sometimes, the stronger the attachment is, the more connection we need to come out of it. We didn't become addicted by accident. It happened because we were hurting and isolated, because we were left to carry things no one should ever have had to carry alone.

So healing takes more than insight. It also requires support, resources, and community. This community needs to be the kind that doesn't just tell you to be strong but also shows up to help you stay tender. Healing, after all, isn't about willpower. It's about connection. And true connection is rooted in safety and sustained by community.

Sacred Pause

For the Ones Learning a New Kind of Comfort

Take a breath. A full, slow breath that belongs only to you.

This pause is for anyone who ever carried an attachment without a connection. It's for anyone who held on to something, whether it was a person, a substance, a behavior, or a belief, not because it was safe, but because it was there.

It's for the ones who stayed with what was familiar, even when it hurt, because it was the only thing that didn't disappear. It's for the ones whose attachments took the form of overworking, people-pleasing, perfectionism, control, disappearing, staying silent, keeping busy, or making themselves small.

It's for the ones who clung to whatever numbed them, because nothing had ever held them gently. And it's for the ones who are still holding on to that now. It's okay to be in both places, to want the comfort of what you've always known, and to long for the kind of safety you've never truly had.

In this pause, stop and remember that your pain made sense. Your reaching for comfort made sense, too. Your body did what it had to do to survive. But you don't have to keep surviving the same way anymore. You're allowed to want more, to need more, and to receive more.

You're allowed to rest in the truth that you were never too broken to be loved, you were just too alone to feel it. Let this breath be the beginning of a new kind of connection.

You are for...

You are for softness that doesn't sting.
For warmth that stays.
For truth that holds, not harms.

You are for reaching without fear.
Needing without shame.
Healing without punishment.

You are for connection that roots you, not tethers you.
For comfort that restores, not controls.
For love that sees all of you and stays.

You are for steadiness.
For relationships that don't require you to shrink.
For safety that doesn't have to be earned.
For belonging that lets you breathe.

You are not too far gone.

You are not too broken.

You are not behind.

You are just beginning to come home.
To yourself.
To your needs.
To the kind of love that doesn't ask you to bleed for it.

Sacred Lesson from True:
From Knots to Warriors

Childhood trauma doesn't just deprive us; it also reprograms us. It interrupts what should have been sacred. What should have been a steady supply of safety and belonging gets invaded by chaos, fear, and confusion. And what's left behind are potholes, places where the ground should have held but gave way instead. Then we wonder why we stumble, why love feels slippery, why peace won't hold, and why we brace for rejection even when we're safe.

Each stage of childhood is meant to offer a foundation. Infancy is a time for being held. Toddlerhood is for exploring our surroundings safely. School age is for asking questions, being seen, and learning to trust our voice. Adolescence is for becoming and belonging. But when trauma enters the picture, those sacred tasks get interrupted. The foundation turns into patchwork, the self becomes fragmented, and we begin to shape our identity not around who we are, but around what we have had to survive.

That's where the "nots" begin: the "not-enough," the "not-lovable," the "not-safe-to-speak," the "not-allowed-to-want," the "not-allowed-to-rest," and the "not-allowed-to-need-too-much." They echo inside our bodies and become etched into our bones and breath. They tighten our throats when we try to speak and curl around our rest and call it laziness. They're so familiar, we begin to mistake them for the truth.

But they are not the truth. They're just survival stories, unfinished ones. And they're waiting to be rewritten.

We can begin this rewriting process by naming the knots, because that's what these "nots" really are: knots held within the body. They're tangles where healthy beliefs became bound with pain. A belief like *I matter* got twisted up with *but only if I'm perfect.* A truth like *I deserve love* became knotted together with *but love hurts.*

When we begin to heal, we can't rip those knots out. We have to disentangle them, gently, tenderly, slowly, and with truth. Sometimes this untangling comes through tears, and other times it happens in silence. It may take place when we say a gentle "no" after only ever saying "yes." It may come in laughter that rises from somewhere sacred and long forgotten. But every time a knot loosens, something true breathes a little more freely.

This book has undone a lot of knots for me. I'd never thought I was creative or that my words mattered. I'd never imagined that my pain had a purpose. For most of my life, I'd only felt like I was too much and not enough all at the same time. Those were my knots, the ones that wrapped around my voice, my worth, and my ability to believe that healing could begin with me.

And still, here I am, writing. My words may not be perfect, but they're true. The girl who once believed her voice didn't matter has finally dared to speak. The woman she became has refused to let silence have the final word.

Even if this book helps only one person, I believe that one person could go on to help a thousand. That's what healing does: it ripples out into the world. One person healing can shift an entire generation. One person coming home to their worth can make it safer for someone else to come home to theirs. That's how it spreads, through love and truth, when someone is brave enough to go first.

Some people are raised with so much love that it lingers around them like a favorite scent. You can sense it in the way they rest, in the way they stick around, and in the way they love without fear. My husband is one of those people. He was loved well. And I'm forever grateful that the universe, and Match.com, brought us together. He carries a kind of peace I've had to fight for. And sometimes, when I forget, I let his love remind me what I deserve.

Some children grow up to become lovers, in the literal sense of people who love, because they were taught how. Some of us instead became warriors because we had to. We fought for safety and the right to survive, sometimes by becoming silent in a world that didn't protect us. We became strong, hyperaware, self-reliant, and unbreakable on the outside while falling apart on the inside.

But healing shows us something sacred. We don't have to live inside armor forever. The body that once braced for every blow can begin to soften. The voice that once stayed silent can begin to sing. And every time we choose love over fear, truth over shame, and connection over protection, we help build a stronger foundation, not only for ourselves but also for every other soul who follows.

The warrior can become a lover. The survivor can become a healer. The child who carried all the "nots" can grow up to teach others what they are really for. This is how we make our story mean something: we live it, heal it, and learn to love who we became in spite of it. After that, we can turn back for the others. That's the warrior's path. That's the ripple effect and the sacred return.

And make no mistake, returning costs something. But what we gain is a life we no longer have to survive. It's a life we're finally allowed to live.

Sacred Pause

For the Lovers and the Warriors

Take a breath here, in through your nose and out through your mouth. Let your shoulders drop, let your belly soften, and let your heart know it's safe to feel.

This pause is for you. It's for the lovers, those who were nurtured in ways that allowed love to take root and bloom without fear. You carry what the world needs most. You offer steadiness without even trying and can show others what it feels like to belong simply by being who you are.

You may not always realize it, but your presence teaches. You are the gift of what went right, and you are needed more than you know.

This pause is also for the warriors, those who grew strong in the absence of safety, who learned to read a room before they ever learned to trust one, and who held the family together or carried secrets too heavy for their age. You survived what tried to steal your voice. You're not here by accident. You're the living proof that healing is possible, even if you're still learning how to live beyond the fight.

This is your reminder: you don't have to stay in survival forever, and you don't have to prove your worth anymore. You don't have to earn what was always meant to be yours: love, rest, safety, belonging, and joy.

Let it ripple through you, just as you are, and out into the world. There will be no more knots, no more pretending, and no more waiting. You are the healer. You are the ripple. You are the return.

You are for...

You are for the slow, sacred undoing.
For every knot unwrapped and every truth recovered.

You are for the strength that softens.

You are for the tenderness that trembles but still shows up.

You are for the legacy-breakers,
the cycle-changers,
the stoic warriors who learn to lay down their armor and pick up love.

You are for sweetness after survival.
For gentleness that doesn't make you weak, but makes you whole.

You are for the stories still being rewritten,
the ones that start with pain but end with power.

You are for becoming the kind of love you never received.
And for recognizing that even when you fall apart, you are already worthy.

You are for rising, not to prove, but to be.
To remember.
To ripple out.
To return.

Sacred Theme Six

Living in Real Time

Sacred Theme Six:
Living in Real Time

Trauma doesn't live only in our memory; it also lives in time. It keeps us stuck in moments that have long passed, reacting to people who aren't even there anymore, reliving pain as if it's still happening now.

But healing brings us back to the present: to our breath, to the moment, and to the life still waiting to be lived.

This theme is about learning how to live in real time again. It's about noticing when the past hijacks the present and gently guiding yourself back with compassion. You can rediscover play as a portal to joy, creativity as a path to aliveness, and presence as your greatest act of resistance.

These lessons invite you to ground yourself, to breathe, and to belong to the present moment because the present is where healing happens and where True lives.

- When the Past Hijacks the Present
- Play Is the Path to Creativity
- Curiosity and Creativity Take Courage

Sacred Lesson from True:
When the Past Hijacks the Present

Sometimes we think we're reacting to what's in front of us. But really, we're reacting to what's behind us, to something we didn't even realize was still there. That's how emotional wounds work. They don't knock politely or wait for our permission. Instead, they come roaring out in moments that look small but feel enormous.

They may show up in traffic, in an argument, or in parenting. They can pop up in the middle of an ordinary Tuesday. And they're not always triggered by obvious things. Sometimes they slip in sideways, making you shut down when someone uses a certain tone of voice. Or they might cause you to panic when someone is five minutes late. You might even dismiss joy before it has a chance to stay, just because joy once ended in pain.

These wounds show up in moments that don't match the size of our reaction because the reaction wasn't born there. It was born long ago.

Here's a moment that caught me off guard. I was walking with three women from my Saturday morning walking group. We chatted and laughed as we strolled along the river, just enjoying the day. One of my friends casually asked, "Hey, where's Jo? I haven't seen her in a while." And before I could even think, my body reacted. I felt a sudden sinking in my stomach and a flash of worry. I found myself thinking, Oh no... did I do something wrong? Is Jo upset with me? Did I mess something up?

It didn't make sense. There was absolutely no reason for me to have such worries. But that didn't matter, because this is what complex post-traumatic stress disorder (C-PTSD) can do. It doesn't wait for logic. It can pull you into old places with familiar fears.

Thankfully, I'd already been in therapy for a while. And before there was time to really start spiraling, I recalled something my therapist had once told me: You've got to bring shame into the light. So I said it out loud, right there on the trail, in the middle of that peaceful morning.

"If y'all want to know what complex PTSD feels like," I said, "you just asked where she was, and my first thought was: Oh no, what did I do?"

They reassured me that it wasn't about me, of course. And I already knew that. But my first thought had nevertheless been that it was about me. It wasn't that I was self-centered; rather, I was ready to blame myself. Unlike my friends, I didn't begin speculating about what was going on with Jo, who might simply have been tired or too busy, but immediately went to shame: it must be something I did.

And in that moment, something softened. By saying it out loud, I brought the shame into the light. That in turn allowed me to walk myself through it and recognize it as a wound rather than the truth.

There have been a lot of moments like that in my life. Hundreds, maybe even thousands of them have occurred. Each time, something went wrong, and I assumed it was because of me: a look, a silence, a mood I couldn't name, a friend not texting back, someone leaving early or not saying goodbye. And my brain filled in the blanks with shame: It's you. You did something wrong. You are something wrong.

Somewhere along the way, I'd learned that if something bad happened, I must have been the reason. And that belief influenced both the way I saw the world and the way I saw myself. That's what trauma does. It makes the past feel like it's always just beneath the surface. It makes the now feel like then.

Sometimes it shows up in the home we swore we'd run differently. The overworked, exhausted mom or dad comes home running on fumes. And the first thing they see that isn't compliance, whether it's a spilled cup, a sibling fight, or a forgotten assignment, gets met with yelling and threats.

In the morning, they might startle their children awake, shouting, "Get up! Let's go! We're going to be late!" When trauma is allowed free rein, there can be no gentleness or breathing room. There's no time to slow down when your body is still responding to the past and the wounds you carry are coloring your world.

And when the emotional flashback passes, you're left in the wreckage, looking around sheepishly at the people you love, whom you may have just startled, hurt, or shut out. And you think, Wow, I guess I'm just the biggest jerk now. I ruined things again.

When you've always been blamed and were never shown how to repair, you assume a breakdown means rejection. You conclude that the moment you mess up, you are the mess. You can't see the wound or the path back, only the damage and a door closing. The worst part is that there's a part of you that agrees with the judgment, believes the shame, and whispers, You always do this. You're just like the people who hurt you. No one's ever going to stick around.

So you armor up and push people away before they can leave. You shut down before they can shame you. And if someone calls you on it, tells you that you hurt them, asks why you're being like this, or says they can't take it anymore, you might snap again. You might respond with coldness, sarcasm, or retreat. Or even worse, you might think, Fine. I'm just the asshole. That's who I am. When you don't know how to come back from a wound, you start believing you are the wound.

But that's not really who you are. That reaction may have come from trauma, from a child part still carrying the weight of every unhealed emotional injury and still waiting for someone to show them a way back. But it is not the whole of who you are.

And here's the sacred truth: you are not the worst thing you've done in pain. You are not your most reactive moment, your sharpest words, your coldest silences, or your fiercest push. You are for repair. You are for returning and healing.

You don't need to live like this, staying stuck in cycles you never chose. You don't have to be an overreactor, the one who's always too much or too sensitive or too angry. You don't have to believe the lie that no one wants to be around you. And you certainly don't need to keep abandoning yourself just to be accepted.

You're not too much. You're not beyond repair. You're a person in pain, still worthy of love and still capable of healing.

And you get to come back, even if your voice trembles with shame, the people you love don't understand, and you're not sure how to begin. You can still heal even if it feels like too much time has passed and you've hurt people or even broken your own heart.

You are for healing. You are for wholeness. You are for finding yourself. And by doing this, you can finally find where you belong. Because you do.

You don't have to earn your way home. You only have to remember that there's a way back. And your True will meet you there.

Sacred Pause

Come Back to Now

Take a breath. A real one. The kind that lets your shoulders relax and finds its way all the way down to your belly.

This pause is for anyone who's ever wondered: *What's wrong with me?* It's for anyone who's ever overreacted and then hated themselves for it, or who's ever sat alone in the shame spiral, convincing themselves they were broken.

This moment is for the ones still living in old survival patterns that make sense when you understand the wounds. It's also for the ones who thought healing meant never losing it again and now feel like failures because sometimes the past still grabs the wheel.

This is your reminder: Flashbacks don't make you unworthy. Reactions don't make you unforgivable. Shame doesn't get the final word. Breathe again and feel the truth of this moment: You are here. You are trying. And you are allowed to come back to yourself again and again.

This moment isn't too late. You're not too far gone.

You are for...

You are for healing.

You are for gentleness.

You are for repair, not just with others, but within yourself.

You are for self-compassion, not self-condemnation. For learning how to stay when everything in you wants to run.

You are for growing new responses where old reactions used to live.

You are for finding your way back.
Back to now.
Back to truth.
Back to the parts of you that were never too much, just too burdened.
Back to the part of you that still believes it's possible to belong.

You are for light.

You are for rest.

You are for beginning again.

Sacred Lesson from True:
Play Is the Path to Creativity

I didn't grow up playing, or in any case, I never engaged in any play that felt free, that made me lose track of time and let my mind wander. Creativity never felt safe, because in my world, nothing was safe. I couldn't freely feel joy, express myself, or indulge in imagination.

So by the time I became a therapist, I didn't think of play as healing. I viewed it only as something for kids. And even then, I considered it to be for kids lucky enough to not already be buried in their efforts to survive.

In 2013, I was a brand-new therapist. I was also a single mom with a full-time job and full-body exhaustion. I was back in school because my student loans were coming due and play therapy classes offered me a way to delay the repayment. I didn't go to heal but to survive. But against all expectations, in doing this, I discovered something sacred.

The first class I took in the play therapy program was taught by Dr. Tessa Hastings, PhD, who is now one of my dearest friends. But back then, she was the first person to see my True before I even knew I had one. She told me once, "Your light is so big." Although I couldn't see it, she could, and I will treasure that forever.

When we walked into class on that first day, a little gingerbread cut-out and four Band-Aids sat on every desk. Tessa told us, "Bandage your person." I had no idea what to do. I looked at the Band-Aids. Four? That's all? I felt uncomfortable, exposed, and confused. But I did it anyway. I put one on the head for the mental abuse, one on the heart for the betrayal and heartbreak, and one on each foot for the years I was frozen in fear.

Then came the question, "What happened to your person?" and a steam train of trauma came barreling forward. I'd spent so much of my life being intellectual and striving to look put together. I could survive anything, so long as I didn't feel it. But play therapy asked me to feel, to be curious, and to explore the parts of myself that I'd spent decades avoiding.

That's when the nightmares started, the ones about things that were never supposed to be spoken of. I was a hot mess. And Tessa saw me. She didn't try to fix me or press me. She just held the space in which True could rise.

And when I began learning about child-centered play, I discovered something bigger than theory. I learned that children play out what they don't have words for. And I remembered that I myself had never played, at least not in a way that felt safe or let me come alive.

Slowly but surely, all these wounded parts of me started surfacing. For years, these little pieces of myself had been waiting to be seen. To be honest, it was miserable at times. I was hypervigilant, dysregulated, and constantly unsure of what was happening. I didn't know how to process it and had no clue what kind of therapy I needed at the time. So I did what I've always done: I rode it out.

But now, all these years later, I can see that this time in my life was the beginning. It was the first crack in the wall that let me wake up to creativity.

I'd never seen myself as creative. My stepdad, who raised me, had been an artist, and my sister was too, but my own efforts to make art or be creative had been dismissed so many times growing up. I'd been laughed at, criticized, and ignored. Even my private diary had been read, filling me with a sense of violation. So how could I trust creativity? How could I offer something that came from the most vulnerable part of me? I didn't know how to create anything sacred without expecting it to be eviscerated.

But now I know that creativity is sacred and begins with curiosity. It grows when there's safety and only blooms when True is allowed to breathe. Now I see play everywhere: in gardening, photography, painting, writing, cooking, coloring, organizing, and even in restoring furniture. Play can happen anytime I forget to be afraid. And when this is the case, I can always feel her, True, rising through my fingertips.

Play isn't a luxury but a necessary language of the soul. It's how we heal what we never got to say. And when you've spent your life shut down, play is how you come back alive.

Sacred Pause

For the Ones Learning to Play Again

Close your eyes. Release the tension in your body and allow your shoulders to drop. Breathe into the space between protection and possibility.

Now whisper: *Play isn't just for children. It's a sacred activity that brings freedom. It's how my True remembers that I'm safe now.*

It's okay if you don't know how to begin. Just be curious. You don't need a paintbrush, a journal, or perfect silence. You just need permission, and True is giving it to you now. You're allowed to color outside the lines. You have the right to dream up stories that don't make sense immediately. Feel free to try and fail and laugh and feel. This is your time to come alive.

Play is not childish but leads you to your homecoming. And you don't need to be unburdened to begin; you just need to be held while you do it.

Let play hold you now.

You are for...

You are for wonder.

You are for boundless curiosity.

You are for creativity that flows without fear.

You are for joy that rises without apology.

You are for moments of aliveness, even if they come slowly.

You are for the kind of play that heals what silence tried to steal.

You are for making things. Messy things. Beautiful things. True things.

You are for breath, for movement, for color and courage and imagination.

You are for returning to the part of you that was never the problem, the part only waiting to be seen.

You are for being fully alive in your own story.

You are for play.

You are for light.

You are for True.

Sacred Lesson from True:
Curiosity and Creativity Take Courage

There's something no one tells you about healing: it requires curiosity and creativity, and both of these things involve vulnerability and the courage to say, I don't have all the answers, but this part of me matters. For those of us who didn't grow up with safety, that kind of courage can feel dangerous.

No one tells you this because most of us were raised in systems that reward obedience while downplaying exploration. Since curiosity threatens control and creativity challenges the rules, they're often discouraged, especially in children who already feel like a burden.

I was about eight when I learned that even a small question like why someone else got an extra pancake could get me in trouble. I was just being curious, but the response taught me everything I needed to know: curiosity wasn't safe. Questions could be punished and silence was safer than asking.

So many of us learned this very early on. Asking "why" could be met with a glare, showing excitement could get you mocked, and wanting to understand made you difficult. So we stopped asking and even stopped wondering. We learned to survive without answers to our questions.

When I began to heal, my curiosity came back slowly, creeping in through education and peeking out in safe spaces where people didn't flinch when I shared an idea. It was nurtured in every moment that said, You're allowed to wonder here.

A Lifespan Development class opened up something new for me. As we studied how people grow and change emotionally, physically, socially, and cognitively across the lifespan, I began to see my own story differently. I realized that many of the struggles I carried made sense in the context of what I had been through. Later, Dr. Barrett's research program gave that curiosity room to breathe. Each safe experience made me braver, and sometimes all it took was a nod, a comment like "That's a great question," or a moment when someone paused and really listened. Safety doesn't always arrive in grand gestures. Sometimes it's just a simple encouragement like "Yes, keep going." And those moments matter more than we know.

Once I started to let my creativity flow, I found that I had so many ideas. Most didn't work, and I'll probably have a million more that don't. But that's what curiosity is. It's permission to explore, not pressure to be perfect. When we have this permission, our curiosity can take root and become a voice. It lets us ask, What if this could be different? It encourages us to sit with a part of ourselves and whisper, What does she need? Then we can begin to build something new, something more loving, something that lasts. Something true.

This book and the first one, You Are for True, have been my arena, my place to whisper, shout, and return. Writing the chapters of You Are for True that cover ages twelve through eighteen nearly broke me. Each one held a truth I had carried in silence for decades. Some days, I didn't think I could keep going. But I did. And that, more than anything, taught me what it means to heal through creation.

At first, I thought I was writing a book to tell my story, but somewhere along the way, it began to tell me who I was. It gave shape to memories I had tried to outrun and gave voice to parts of me that were still afraid to speak. And in doing so, it gave me back to myself.

I don't claim to own the truth. I say only, "I bring something, and what I bring matters." And what you bring matters, too. That could be your ideas and dreams or your notes scribbled on napkins. They all matter. You don't have to be published, polished, or perfect to create something sacred. You just have to begin. Let your True come through in whatever way she chooses.

Here's what I want you to remember: there's no such thing as courage without fear. They walk together, always. Fear shows up with the unknown and the vulnerable voice that says, This might go wrong. But courage says, Let's get support. Let's gather knowledge. Let's do it anyway.

Courage is feeling scared but moving forward anyway, with your scared parts in your arms. So honor both of these things: the part of you that was terrified and the part of you that showed up anyway.

Keep in mind that you're doing things today that your ten-year-old self never thought possible. You're allowed to grow, change, and take a new direction. You are for healing. You are for creating. You are for becoming. You are for True.

This isn't easy work, but you're doing it. Even reading this book is an act of courage, an act of reclaiming your voice, your path, and your sacred light. Let that be enough today. Let that be everything.

And if you ever forget, come back to this page. Take another breath with your hand over your heart. And never forget that the courage it took to arrive here is the same courage that will carry you forward.

You're not alone. You're not too late. You're not too much. You're ready.

You are for True. And True is for you.

Sacred Pause

A Moment for the Brave Ones

Close your eyes, just for a breath. Let yourself feel the quiet underneath the noise.

You've taken in a lot. You've walked through memories and stayed with words that once felt too big. And that matters. You don't have to create anything right now. You don't have to solve anything or be brilliant or brave or sure. You just get to rest here.

So rest now, in this moment, alone with your breath, your heartbeat, and the truth that healing doesn't require perfection, it only asks for presence.

Take one more breath, softly and slowly. Let it remind your body that you are safe now. You are not behind, and curiosity is welcome here.

When you're ready, open your eyes gently and know that simply being here is enough.

You are for...

You are for curiosity that leads you back home.

You are for creativity that rises from your healing.

You are for the wonderings that never stopped asking *What if?*

You are for the sacred things that only you can bring to life.

You are for the courage it takes to begin again.

You are for the softness beneath your strength.

You are for scribbles, for whispers, for all the unfinished beauty inside you.

You are for stories that unfold in your own time.

You are for becoming, for remembering, for returning.

You are for healing that tells the truth.

You are for creating what has never been created before, because no one else is you.

You are for True.

And True is for you.

Sacred Theme Seven

When Everything Falls Away, You Remain

Sacred Theme Seven:
When Everything Falls Away, You Remain

There are seasons in life that don't announce themselves as transformations but instead arrive in the form of loss, collapse, or grief. They look like failure from the outside and feel like unraveling from the inside. And yet, when the roles fall away and the identities we have built to survive finally come undone, something unexpected is revealed. What is left is neither emptiness nor nothingness, but truth. What is left is you.

This final theme was not originally planned but emerged from things I experienced. I didn't find them by looking back at healed places, as with the other ones, but from standing in the middle of the storm and choosing to stay anyway. They are the rawest of all the lessons in this book, because they're the most recent. The wounds here are still tender, and the grief is still learning how to breathe. But that's exactly why they belong here.

Healing happens in its own time, rather than when we're ready to write about it. It comes in the closing of practices and the burying of fathers and the small, still moments when we finally ask who we are when there is no one left to perform for. It arrives when we stop measuring our worth by what a thimble can hold and begin to understand, for the first time, that we have always been the ocean.

These lessons are for anyone standing in the middle of their own falling away. They're for the ones who have lost something they built with their own hands, who are grieving an identity that no longer fits them, and who are learning, slowly and bravely, what remains when everything else is gone. What remains is you. And you have never needed to earn the chance for a new beginning.

- A Thimble Cannot Measure an Ocean
- Identity Is More than the Roles You Play
- Sometimes Knowing What You Don't Want Is Enough

Sacred Lesson from True:
A Thimble Cannot Measure an Ocean

There comes a time when your body begins telling the truth before your mind is ready to hear it. It may show up as exhaustion, irritability, numbness, or a sudden urge to pull away from something you've been trying desperately to hold together. And if you've spent your life believing that love is proven through endurance, you will likely ignore those signals. You may push harder, stay longer, and convince yourself that you should be able to handle more.

For most of my life, I believed that these behaviors were signs of strength. I had to confront and reconsider that belief when my dad was dying. We didn't have a relationship. We hadn't spoken in four years, and even before that, there had never been a deep sense of connection between us. He left when I was a baby, and I didn't meet him again until I was fifteen. I lived most of my life without him. Even after we reconnected, I often felt as though I was standing beside someone who could see me but would never truly know me.

Toward the end of his life, I learned he was dying of cancer. But I didn't reach out to him, even months after finding out. For a long time, I wasn't sure what to do. Part of me thought I should call, that a good daughter would call. There seemed to be an unspoken expectation that I would become the loving daughter at the end of the story, that somehow the final chapter would make sense of everything that had come before it. But that wasn't my truth.

The truth was that we didn't have that kind of relationship. We weren't estranged because of a fight or a misunderstanding; we were simply disconnected because there had never really been a foundation to return to. I couldn't manufacture feelings I didn't genuinely have, and I couldn't force a connection that had never really existed. What I felt was far more complicated than that.

I did love him, and I hurt for him. I wished things had been different. But I was also angry, disappointed, and exhausted by decades of hoping for something that had never arrived. I didn't know what to do with all of those contradictory feelings coexisting inside me.

I'd tried for years to explain something simple to my dad: the fact that we didn't have a relationship, and I didn't feel connected to him. But every attempt seemed to stop at the surface. He could never hear what I was actually saying. For a long time, I interpreted that as unwillingness on his part, but I eventually came to see it differently. Truly hearing what I was telling him would have required a level of emotional capacity he simply didn't have.

Some people move through the world with the capacity of a thimble because no one ever taught them to hold more. Until they begin building that capacity, they can only give what they were given, see what they were shown, and love as far as they were loved. My father was a thimble. Small not in spirit, but in emotional capacity. He couldn't hold what he had never been taught to carry.

That realization was painful because it forced me to let go of hope. Although I already knew he would never change, I still longed to find some combination of words that would finally at least make him understand.

In the end, I went to see him anyway. By the time I arrived, he was unconscious and nonresponsive. I stayed for three days in my brother's home while my father lay dying in the next room. I helped my sister-in-law care for him. I sat with what was happening and showed up as fully as I could.

But something inside me kept reaching its limit. Although I cared about him, there was no relationship to rest inside of. There was no mutuality, there had never been any repair, and there was certainly no place for my grief to land and find comfort. There was only history, unfulfilled longing, and the reality of what would never be.

Before I left, I sat beside him one last time and said what I needed to say. I told him he had been created to be loved, and that I was sorry no one had ever taught him that. He couldn't hear me, but I needed to say it anyway.

As I drove away, something became clear in a way I had never been able to see before. His lack of capacity had always made me feel that I wasn't enough. Not enough to stay for, or to reach for, or to repair with. For years, I'd carried that story around with me without realizing it wasn't mine.

I could also see where I made the mistake of measuring my ocean by what fit inside him. That is what children do. We look at what someone offers us and decide it must be the most we deserve. We never consider that their container is simply too small. We just think, I must be too much. It doesn't occur to us that the person never learned to hold more. Instead, we think, I must not be worth more than this. But an ocean cannot be measured by a thimble. Your worth cannot be determined by someone else's lack of capacity to see it. You have always been worth much more than a thimbleful of love.

Healing allowed me to see a different truth. My father's inability to really see me had never been evidence that I was unworthy of being seen. His inability to repair had never been proof that I was unworthy of repair. And his inability to love me in the way I needed had never meant I was unlovable. It simply reflected the limits of what he himself could carry, understand, and give. He was a thimble trying to hold an ocean, and that was never a reflection of the ocean. It was only ever a reflection of the thimble.

That realization brought grief with it: grief for the father I lost, and also grief for the father I'd never had. It was grief for the conversations that would never take place, the relationship I'd kept hoping might appear if I just waited long enough, and the little girl who'd spent years believing she simply needed to be more lovable.

But grief also brought clarity. As I drove away, I realized something else. Whatever had happened between my father and me didn't have to become the next chapter of my family's story. My children would never spend years wondering whether they were loved. They would never have to guess where they stood with me or question whether they mattered. I was determined that they would always know it from my words, my presence, and all the ordinary moments that make up a life.

That doesn't mean I've been a perfect parent. It just means I've remained committed to repair. I have continued doing my own work so that my wounds won't become their inheritance. I want my children to experience something I never had: the certainty that even when relationships become strained, love remains available and healthy repair remains possible.

Capacity became personal. While I was learning about my father's limitations, I was also being confronted with my own. There had been moments during those three long days when I'd needed to step away, when I hadn't been able to sit in that room any longer. Times when my body had said, this is enough for now.

In the past, I would have judged myself for that, interpreting those limits as a weakness. I might have assumed I wasn't loving enough, trying hard enough, or staying long enough. But healing taught me something different.

Capacity isn't about how much we can endure but how much we can hold while remaining connected to ourselves. Endurance often asks us to override the signals we receive from our bodies, while capacity urges us to listen to them. Endurance says, keep going no matter the cost. Capacity asks what we can carry without abandoning ourselves in the process. These distinctions changed the way I understood healing.

People don't belong in perpetual punishment. We are all allowed to grow and change. We are allowed to heal, even when it has taken us longer than we wished it had, or when no one ever showed us how, or when we are only now beginning to understand.

Capacity cannot be forced. It has to be built. It grows each time we stay present with something difficult without abandoning ourselves, and each time we choose compassion over shame. It also grows whenever we allow an old wound to be seen, understood, and loved instead of keeping it hidden.

And this process takes time. Capacity is built slowly but surely, as the wounds of the past are uncovered and allowed to heal in love. It happens when we gently return to our bodies, reconnect with truth, and find ourselves again.

Healing isn't measured by how much we can carry. It also has to do with how gently we learn to carry ourselves.

Sacred Pause

For the Ones Who Were Measured by the Wrong Container

Take a breath. Let it reach all the way down into the places that still ache from being unseen. You don't have to rush past those places today. You are allowed to sit with what was lost, what was never given, and what you spent years trying to earn from someone who simply didn't have it to give.

This pause is for the child in you who decided she wasn't enough because the people who were supposed to love her didn't have the capacity. It is for the grown woman who still flinches or wonders sometimes, still catches herself trying to earn something from people who are working with thimbles while she is an ocean.

You were never too much. You were never too needy. You were never unworthy of being held. You were simply in the presence of someone whose capacity couldn't meet yours. And that is their story to carry, not yours.

Place your hand over your heart. Let this be the moment when you stop measuring your worth by what someone else couldn't give. Let yourself feel the size of what you actually are.

You cannot fit into a thimble.
You never could.

You are for...

You are for love that is big enough to hold all of you, not just the parts that are easy.

You are for people whose capacity grows toward yours, not away from it.

You are for the grief of what was never given and the freedom that comes when you stop waiting for it.

You are for seeing clearly, for noticing the limitations of others and the depth of yourself.

You are for handing something different down, a legacy of presence, repair, and love that doesn't ask you to shrink to fit inside it.

You are for the ocean you have always been.

And you are for True, who knew your depth long before you did.

Sacred Lesson from True:
Identity Is More than the Roles You Play

I spent most of my life collecting evidence that I wasn't enough. I felt like a bad mother on my worst days and an inadequate wife on others. In my family of origin, I had long carried the unspoken label of the black sheep, the one who didn't quite fit, and I felt the weight of that difference without ever fully understanding why. I didn't have language for any of it back then. I only knew that I moved through the world with a persistent sense that something essential was missing in me.

Then I became a therapist. Getting my license felt so different from anything I'd ever experienced before. This achievement wasn't handed to me and couldn't be taken away by someone else's mood or opinion. I had studied for it and earned it. For the first time in my life, I had something solid to stand on. I'd poured everything I had into entering that career, reading every book and completing every training. I'd studied relentlessly and done my very best, because this was the thing that finally made sense of my story. It was, I felt, what made me matter.

What I couldn't see then was that I still hadn't found myself. I'd only found a better role to disappear into. My burnout happened during the first six months of my marriage, and it was also in that same period that I began to realize something I hadn't anticipated: my husband loved me in a way that was consistent and safe. And that was deeply unsettling, because safety was unfamiliar territory for me. I didn't know how to receive it or trust it. I couldn't figure out how to be fully present in a real marriage while also being married to my career. Something had to give. The burnout was my body's way of telling me I had been trying to live in two places at once.

I ended up on my own therapist's couch, which is a humbling place for a therapist to be. His name was Nick, and he became one of the most important people in my healing journey. Somewhere in that work, Nick asked me who I was when I wasn't healing others. The room got very quiet, as I hadn't been expecting a question like that. I didn't have an answer at first.

But finally, I told him the truth I'd been carrying around without fully realizing it: if I couldn't be a therapist, I didn't want to live anymore. And I meant it. I didn't want to die, of course, but I just had no idea who I was outside of that role. I wasn't a person who also happened to be a therapist. I was a therapist, and nothing else. Rather than giving me a sense of self, this role had replaced the self I'd never built. This is what role confusion looks like when it goes unaddressed for decades.

One of the most important developmental tasks we face as human beings is discovering who we are. Developmental psychologist Erik Erikson called this stage Identity versus Role Confusion, and although it is most often associated with adolescence, I have come to believe that many of us spend an entire lifetime working through it. Some of the most profound identity work I have witnessed hasn't been in teenagers at all, but in adults who had spent decades living according to expectations, responsibilities, and survival patterns before finally asking themselves a simple question: Who am I?

When most people think about identity, they think about labels: occupations, relationship statuses, personality traits, accomplishments, or affiliations. We introduce ourselves to new acquaintances by telling them what we do, who we love, where we work, or what we have achieved. Yet identity goes much deeper than any of those things. Identity is not a title, a role, or a collection of accomplishments. Rather, it is the continuous sense of self that exists beneath all of it.

For those of us who grew up in environments where survival was the priority, identity development can become especially complicated. Instead of asking, "Who am I?" we often learn to ask, "Who do I need to be?" We become what our families need, what keeps the peace, earns approval, sidesteps criticism, prevents conflict, or protects us from rejection. These adaptations are often brilliant, helping us survive circumstances that would otherwise overwhelm us. The problem is that when survival becomes the focus, authenticity is often postponed.

As a therapist, I have watched this happen over and over again. A woman sits across from me and is easily able to tell me everything about her responsibilities. She can describe her marriage, her children, her career, her aging parents, and the endless demands that life has placed upon her. She knows what everyone else needs and expects. Yet when I ask what she wants, the room often becomes quiet. She genuinely does not know. Somewhere along the way, she became so skilled at adapting that she stopped checking in with herself.

I understand this silence because I myself have lived it. For much of my life, I knew exactly who I needed to be. I knew how to be responsible and helpful, how to work hard. I knew how to care for others, how to achieve, and how to handle more than my share. What I did not know was where those roles ended and I began.

The challenge with role confusion is that it rarely feels confusing while we are living it. In fact, we often feel we have succeeded in life. The caretaker is praised for caring, the achiever is rewarded for achieving, and the helper is appreciated for helping. The strong one becomes the person everyone depends upon. People notice our success in these roles and admire us for it. It may even become the very thing people love most about us. Yet beneath it all, we may become more and more distant from ourselves. Over time, we might begin to mistake the role for our identity. We might forget that being needed isn't the same as being known, and that being useful isn't the same as being authentic. This matters because identity is not simply another developmental milestone but the foundation for every stage that follows.

Erikson proposed that after Identity versus Role Confusion comes Intimacy versus Isolation, and I do not think this sequence is accidental. Before we can truly share ourselves with another person, we must first know ourselves. Otherwise, what we bring into relationships is not intimacy but adaptation. In other words, we try to become who we think our partners need us to be. We silence parts of ourselves to maintain connection, and we shape-shift, accommodate, and perform. The relationship may appear close from the outside, but internally we often feel unseen, because the person our partner is loving is not fully us. True intimacy requires vulnerability, and vulnerability requires identity. We cannot share a self we do not know.

The same principle continues throughout the remaining stages of life. Later, Erikson described the task of Generativity versus Stagnation, a stage focused on contribution, purpose, mentorship, and legacy. Yet contribution becomes complicated when it emerges from role confusion rather than identity. We may spend years caring for others, helping others, rescuing others, or sacrificing for others, all the while hoping that our usefulness will prove our worth. What looks like purpose from the outside may actually be an attempt to earn belonging.

Eventually we arrive at Erikson's final stage: Integrity versus Despair. This is the time when we look back over our lives and make peace with the story we have lived. It is the stage where we ask ourselves whether we have lived authentically or merely performed the roles we believed were expected of us. It is difficult to experience integrity when we have spent decades disconnected from ourselves. Making peace with a life that never truly felt like our own is no easy task.

If we look at it this way, we can see how identity influences every relationship we build, every contribution we make, and every meaning we assign to our lives. It shapes how we love, lead, parent, work, and ultimately how we understand ourselves. Perhaps that is why so many adults find themselves revisiting a question they thought was only for teenagers: "Who am I, really? Who am I when I'm not busy helping, fixing, rescuing, achieving, or proving? Who am I underneath all of that?"

Healing, I have come to believe, is often the process of separating identity from adaptation. It is the gradual work of loosening the roles that once helped us survive so we can discover what remains beneath them. The answer is rarely found all at once. Rather, it emerges slowly through boundaries, grief, honesty, courage, and self-reflection. It appears when we choose authenticity over performance, stop abandoning ourselves to maintain connection, and finally ask what feels true instead of what feels expected.

The question is this: when the roles fall away, what remains? Because the answer to that question will determine every chapter that follows.

Sacred Pause

For the Ones Who Lost Themselves in the Doing

Take a breath. The kind that reminds your body that it's still here, still yours.

Think for a moment about all the roles you have filled. The helper. The strong one. The responsible one. The one everyone called when things fell apart. You wore those roles so long they started to feel like your skin. And maybe no one ever stopped to ask what was underneath them, because you were so good at wearing them.

This pause is for the part of you that got left behind in all that doing, the part that never got to answer the question of who she actually was, because there was always someone who needed something first. She is still in there. She has been waiting patiently all this time.

You don't have to know exactly who you are today. You only have to be willing to ask. Place your hand over your heart and stay here for just a moment. Let this be the beginning of that question, without any pressure to answer it.

You are allowed to not know yet.
That is the most honest place to begin.

You are for...

You are for a life that belongs to you, not just to the people who need you.

You are for the slow, tender work of finding out what you actually want, what you actually feel, and what you actually believe when no one is asking anything of you.

You are for relationships where you don't have to perform your worth or disappear to keep the peace.

You are for the question that scared you most: who are you when the roles fall away?

You are for the answer, wherever the search for it leads and however long it takes to find.

You are for True. And she has been waiting for you to come home to her all along.

Sacred Lesson from True:
Sometimes Knowing What You Don't Want Is Enough

When I finished writing You Are for True, I thought the hardest part was over. For years, I had carried stories around that didn't belong to me, stories about my childhood, my survival, my shame, and the ways I had learned to navigate the world. Writing the book felt like finally telling the truth. I believed that once the truth was spoken, I would feel relief. Instead, it felt like I'd opened a door that could no longer be closed.

Once I sent the manuscript to the editor in June, my nervous system collapsed. As a therapist, I thought I could handle it. After all, I understood trauma, grief, and attachment wounds. I knew how the nervous system worked. What I didn't understand was that knowing something professionally and living through it personally are two very different things. Writing the book stirred up decades of pain, grief, anger, and loss that I'd spent years trying to understand but had never fully allowed myself to feel. The months that followed were some of the darkest of my life. I had panic attacks. I called in sick. I canceled appointments with clients. Some days it took everything I had simply to function. I remember feeling confused by the intensity of it all. I'd expected freedom and relief, but instead felt like I was unraveling. Looking back now, I think my body was finally demanding payment for the unseen truths it had held for decades. The stories had been written. Now they had to be felt.

It was in that period that I signed up for an intensive. I knew something deeper was happening inside me, and I could no longer think my way through it. I needed something more than insight. I needed experience. What I didn't know when I registered was how much my life would change before I arrived.

While waiting for the intensive, I made the difficult decision to close my group practice. Although the choice was ultimately mine, it was still painful. The truth is that I had built much of that business on people-pleasing, conflict avoidance, over-functioning, and poor boundaries. At the time, those patterns looked like evidence of dedication. They seemed to prove my sacrifice and leadership. What I couldn't see was how much of myself I had lost in the process.

Somewhere along the way, I had become responsible for everything: everyone else's problems, emotions, and conflicts. I spent more time managing personalities than actually doing the work I loved. I hadn't gone to graduate school to investigate which staff member had stolen another's lunch from the refrigerator. I hadn't become a therapist so I could remind fully grown adults to replace the toilet paper, flush the toilet, or clean up after themselves. Yet somehow that had become a big part of my life.

When I finally made that decision, I drove away from my office with a feeling I can only describe as unbearable. I felt like I didn't deserve to breathe the same air as everyone else. I felt ashamed, embarrassed, and humiliated, like a failure and a joke at the same time. Worse, I felt like I had somehow become the lesson everyone else got to learn from while I was the one who had to live it.

The intensive was scheduled for the following weekend. When I'd registered, I still had a company. By the time I arrived, my nervous system had collapsed, my identity felt shattered, and I was grieving the loss of a dream I had spent years building. I walked into that intensive with a far heavier load than I had intended.

One of the exercises involved something called body mapping. As we worked through the process, we were asked to write down the beliefs we uncovered. Some of them I knew well, while others surprised me. One by one, I wrote them down and then attached the paper to a punching bag lying on the floor. I remember looking at the words on that bag.

My body isn't my own.

That one stopped me immediately. Then there were others.

I'm a failure. I'm nothing.

These beliefs had silently followed me around for years, influencing the way I saw myself and the choices I made.

At the end of the exercise, the therapist handed me a bat. At first, I felt ridiculous. My husband was there supporting me, and the therapist was watching. Part of me wanted to laugh and say, "I'm not doing that." Instead, I looked back down at the words on the bag, and something inside me broke open. I started swinging.

I hit that punching bag again and again, until the years of grief, anger, shame, and fatigue began pouring out of me. Suddenly, I no longer cared who was watching. I stopped trying to look composed. As I swung that bat, I stopped being the therapist in the room and became the woman underneath all of it, the daughter, the wounded child, the exhausted caretaker, the business owner who felt like a failure, the woman who had spent a lifetime trying to earn her worth. I kept swinging until I had pounded all those old beliefs into oblivion. At last, in tears and exhausted, I realized there was nothing left.

At one point, in the middle of it, I heard a strange sound. It sounded almost like someone laughing. I wondered who it was before realizing it was actually coming from me. But it wasn't laughter. It was pain, raw and unfiltered, finally finding its way to the surface after years of being trapped inside me. The tears that came at the end were the kind that come from somewhere so deep you don't know how to stop them.

My husband wrapped his arms around me and held me while I sobbed, and he didn't try to fix anything or reassure me. His simple presence in that moment was exactly what I needed.

Looking back now, I don't think the most important thing happened while I was swinging the bat. I think it happened afterward. As I stood there crying, something began to shift within me. For perhaps the first time in my life, I understood that I was being loved exactly as I was. I hadn't had to "earn" this love by fixing everything, rebuilding my life, redeeming myself, or proving I could put all the pieces back together. In that moment, while my life felt like a car crash that would never stop, I was being loved right in the middle of the mess.

What made that realization so powerful was that some of the circumstances I was grieving had been created by my own choices: the people-pleasing, the poor boundaries, the conflict avoidance, the patterns I'd spent a lifetime repeating. I wasn't simply grieving things that had happened to me. I was also grieving things I had participated in bringing about. And somehow, I was still worthy of compassion. That may have been the most sacred lesson of all.

For most of my life, I'd believed that love had to be earned, that nobody was ever loved unless they achieved things, sacrificed themselves, helped others, and generally got things right. That day, I learned something different. Love was never waiting for me on the other side of perfection. It was sitting beside me in the rubble all along.

Still, the crash didn't stop there. Over the following months, I finished the difficult work of closing my practice. Clients transitioned, doors closed, and chapters ended. Then in March, my father died.

I put this book on hold at that time because I felt like a fraud writing about healing while living through my own identity crisis. I kept thinking I needed to have it all figured out before I could finish it. I know now that healing doesn't work that way. It doesn't always happen at the end of a storm; it sometimes comes when you're still standing in the middle of it.

For a long time, I thought wisdom meant knowing exactly what I wanted. I did know that I wanted certainty, a plan, a clear picture of the future. What this period in my life taught me was that sometimes clarity arrives in a different form. Sometimes we discover what we don't want long before we discover what we do. I learned that I didn't want a life built on self-abandonment. I didn't want success that depended on carrying everyone else's responsibilities. And I certainly didn't want fear making decisions for me. Those realizations didn't tell me exactly where I was going, but they did show me where I could no longer stay. And sometimes that's enough of a starting point.

More than a year has passed since I sent that manuscript to the editor. The group practice is now gone. My father is gone. Many of the identities I spent years building have fallen away along with them. And now I find myself standing in a new office with a key in my hand, preparing to begin again. Only this time, it feels different.

I'm no longer trying to build something because I think I should. I'm not trying to prove anything anymore, or measuring my worth by how much I can carry, fix, save, or sacrifice. Instead, I'm learning something much simpler. I'm learning how to be myself. That may sound like a small thing, but for someone who spent a lifetime becoming what other people needed, it feels revolutionary.

The truth is that I still don't know exactly what comes next. I'm still learning, growing, making mistakes, and finding my way. More losses certainly lie ahead. There will be times in the future when I get it wrong. Being human guarantees that. But the sacred lesson I carry with me now is this: my worth isn't riding in the car that crashes. It isn't destroyed if my nervous system collapses. It isn't obliterated if I close a practice. It doesn't disappear into the ground if I bury someone. And it won't be demolished by whatever comes next, either.

For years, I thought healing meant rebuilding myself into someone better. Now I think it may be about finally having the courage to discover who I was beneath everything I had learned to become. As I prepare to unlock the door to a new office and begin again, I am finally giving myself permission to simply be me, because as it turns out, I was the center of my own story all along.

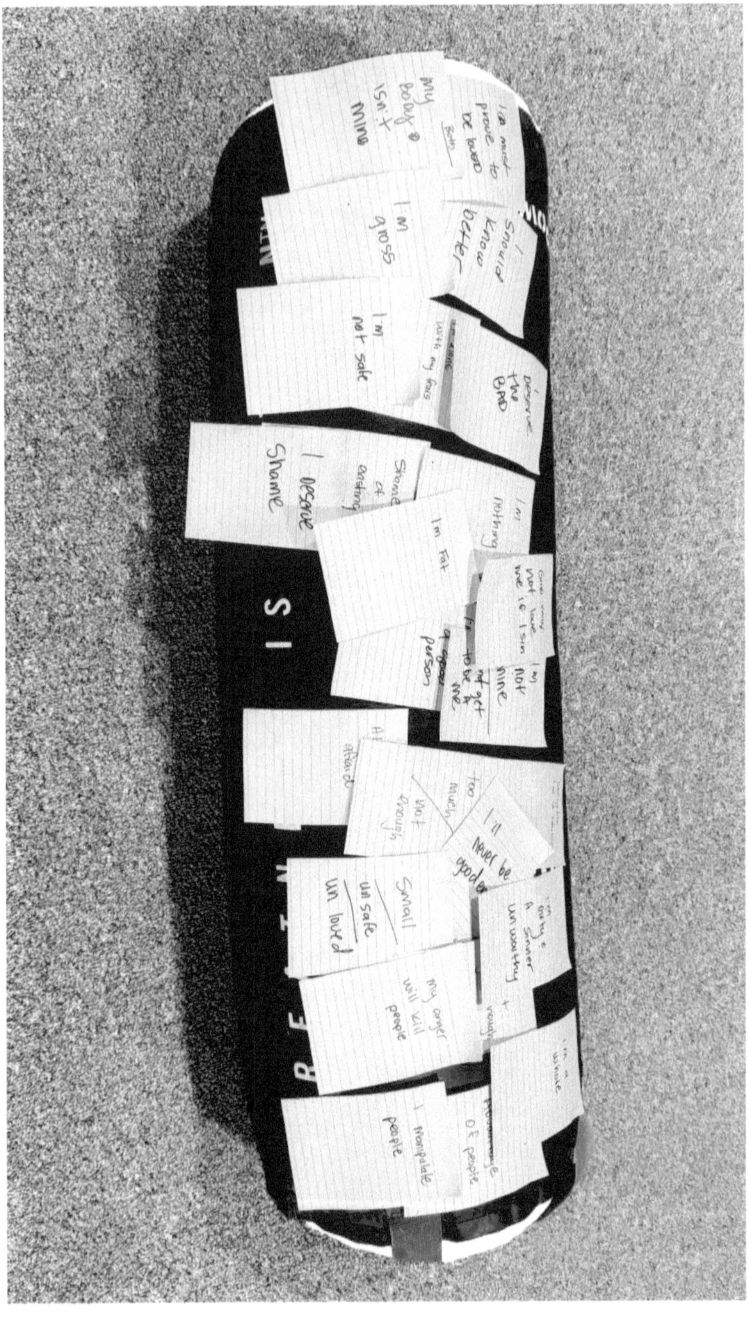

I had carried these beliefs so long, I didn't even realize how many there were until I saw them all in front of me.

Sacred Pause

For the Ones Who Are Beginning Again

Take a slow breath. Let it reach the places that are still tender, the places that held the grief of what was lost, the dream that didn't survive, the version of yourself you had to let go of before you were ready.

You are allowed to grieve all of it. Projects you've had to end, identities that weren't right for you, and people you've lost. The version of your life you thought you were building. Grief doesn't mean you failed. It means something mattered. You're allowed to let it matter while also letting it go.

This pause is for anyone who has ever stood at the beginning of something new and felt more terrified than hopeful. For anyone who has closed a door they built with their own hands and wondered if they had the strength to open another one. For anyone who has learned something about themselves the hard way, through collapse rather than clarity, through loss rather than choice.

You aren't starting over.

You're starting from everything you now know.

And that's not the same thing at all.

You are for...

You are for the version of success that doesn't cost you yourself.

You are for love that holds you on good days or bad.

You are for clarity that comes slowly and honestly, through the wreckage of what no longer fits.

You are for beginning again, not because you have to, but because something true in you refuses to stay where it no longer belongs.

You are for the new office, the new key, and the small revolution of simply being yourself.

You are for True. And this time, you are building something with her, not instead of her.

A FINAL NOTE FROM ME

When I wrote *You Are for True*, I was finally telling the truth about what happened to me. When I began writing this book, I thought I was simply going back through those stories to share what they had taught me. I didn't know that life would hand me new lessons before I could finish it.

This book followed me through loss, grief, endings, and the unraveling of identities I had spent years building. There were times when I put it away because I no longer felt qualified to write about healing. I was still hurting. I was still confused. I was still trying to find my way through a life that no longer looked the way I thought it would.

But maybe that is part of what makes these lessons sacred. They were not written from the other side of a perfectly finished healing journey. They were written while I was still living it.

If you have found pieces of your own story in these pages, I hope you know you do not have to have everything figured out before you begin. You do not have to become less tender, less complicated, or less human to be worthy of love. You are allowed to grieve what happened to you and what never got to happen for you. You are allowed to outgrow the roles that once helped you survive. You are allowed to discover who you are beneath everything you learned to become.

Most of all, I hope these pages have helped you see that what happened to you was never the whole truth about you. There is still a self beneath the shame, the fear, the grief, and the armor. That self was never gone. It may have been hidden, protected, or waiting for enough safety to grow, but it was still there.

I cannot tell you exactly what your healing will look like or where it will lead. I can only tell you what I have learned along the way: you were never created merely to survive your life. You were created to be loved, respected, protected, celebrated, and known. You were created to belong to yourself.

Thank you for allowing me to share these sacred lessons with you. I hope they help you recognize some of your own.

Stay tender. Stay true. Stay you.

Melanie

ABOUT MELANIE TAYLOR

Melanie Taylor is a Licensed Professional Counselor-Supervisor, author, and therapist specializing in complex trauma and complex PTSD. Her work explores how childhood experiences shape the way we understand ourselves, navigate relationships, and move through the world. She is especially interested in the social, emotional, and relational capacities that may be interrupted by trauma and can continue developing throughout adulthood.

Melanie is the author of *You Are for True* and *Sacred Lessons from True*. Through her writing, she weaves personal storytelling with what she has learned as a therapist and as a woman doing her own healing work. Her approach is grounded in the belief that understanding what happened to us matters, but healing also requires opportunities to experience safety, develop a relationship with ourselves, and discover who we are beneath the roles and protective patterns we learned to carry.

In her clinical practice, Melanie offers private therapy intensives for adults who want focused, uninterrupted space to work through complex trauma, painful patterns, and experiences that may be difficult to reach in traditional weekly sessions. She also supervises developing counselors and creates practical training and experiential resources for therapists through Red Couch Learning, which she co-founded with Dr. Tessa Hastings.

Melanie lives in Arkansas with her husband, Andy. When she is not writing, teaching, or sitting on the other side of the therapy room, she is usually dreaming up a new way to make what feels invisible easier to see.

Stay tender. Stay true. Stay you.

CONTINUE THE JOURNEY

To learn more about working with me, therapy intensives, TRUE Clarity Sessions, and upcoming resources and trainings, visit www.youarefor.com or email me at melanie@youarefor.com.

www.ingramcontent.com/pod-product-compliance
Lightning Source LLC
LaVergne TN
LVHW100731061126
851857LV00011B/485
* 9 7 9 8 9 9 3 8 6 4 8 2 2 *